MA

THE CLASSIC CHILDREN'S TV QUIZ BOOK

THE CLASSIC CHILDREN'S TV QUIZ BOOK

Compiled by Dean Wilkinson

Foreword by Ant McPartlin and Dec Donnelly

APEX PUBLISHING LTD

First published in 2008 by

Apex Publishing Ltd

PO Box 7086, Clacton on Sea, Essex, CO15 5WN, England

www.apexpublishing.co.uk

Copyright © 2008 by Dean Wilkinson
The author has asserted his moral rights

British Library Cataloguing-in-Publication Data
A catalogue record for this book
is available from the British Library

ISBN HARDBACK: 1-906358-25-7   978-1-906358-25-9

Typeset in 10.5pt Chianti Bdlt Win95BT

Production Manager: Chris Cowlin

Cover Design: Siobhan Smith

Printed and bound in Great Britain by the
MPG Books Group, Bodmin and King's Lynn

In memory of Mark Speight 1965 – 2008, whom Timmy and I had the

enormous pleasure of working with on Timmy Towers.

A great talent, a great bloke and a

great loss to children's television.

www.speightoftheart.org

INTRODUCTION
By Dean Wilkinson

Working largely in children's telly since 1990, I've clocked up a few shows myself and modesty prevents me from including any of them in this tome - one would have thought! You'll find SMTV Live and Stupid in here somewhere. I'm really proud of these shows, especially Stupid, and when I snuff it I want there to be a headline in my local paper stating 'STUPID MAN DIES'.

The emphasis of this quiz book seems to be the children's telly of the seventies and eighties. This is because I was a kid myself at that time spending hours upon hours watching the haunted fish tank trying to escape from the reality of a grim home life. And wow, was I spoilt for choice - so many classics! and I've enjoyed all of those shows again whilst researching this book, either by hiring them from Amazon, bidding for the last tatty VHS versions on Ebay, or seeking out clips on You Tube.

The American wit Lily Tomlin once said: 'If you read a lot of books you are considered well read, but if you watch a lot of TV you are not considered well viewed.'

Depends on the telly, Lily. I'd much rather spend an evening in front of a DVD copy of Children of the Stones or Dangermouse or Maid Marian and her Merry Men than doing anything else. I spent half my childhood watching telly, I wasted the rest, so I'm spending my adult life catching up.

I've trawled the Internet, scoured books on TV history and bugged friends and colleagues in the biz for their memories, to make this the ultimate classic children's telly quiz book. I hope I've succeeded.

Even if you don't remember the show, you can get a lot out of the *DID YOU KNOW?* sections, or glean amazing nuggets of information about kids' telly by cheating and looking at the *ANSWERS* in the back. Impress your friends with some impromptu facts about Willo the Wisp, or The Double Deckers.

I hope you'll come to realise, like I did when compiling this book, that as a kid I was incredibly lucky to have such a wide and varied choice of viewing.

But, now I'm a dad I find it heartbreaking that the children's telly my daughters have to choose from is - colossal because of the myriad cable channels on offer, but - incredibly limited in terms of quality. There's some really awful acquired American kids' telly around. Really really awful!

Not all of it though! I've included the fairly modern Spongebob in this book because it's a great example of superbly crafted telly for kids, AND it follows the golden rule, kids' telly should entertain adults too. And the American Eerie Indiana was one of the best shows of the 1990s.

I'm a true Brit and we have got to get British children's telly back into gear. Just look at the multitude of superbly made, (sometimes without much of a budget), imaginative and downright awe inspiring shows mentioned in this book. Catweazle, Worzel Gummidge, Do Not Adjust Your Set, Thunderbirds, The Ghosts of Motley Hall - gosh the list was so huge I simply could not cram in every show I wanted to! We have to get back those glorious must-see-TV days!

If the British television executives stopped wasting cash on banal rubbish and put the resources into good children's telly, they could double, even treble their viewing figures! And our youth might grow up with a sense of magical wonder instead of the feelings of desperation, bitchiness and avarice that modern telly bestows upon them. Look at any of today's pointless celebrities and their God awful vehicles and just think about what they're saying to our young people. The messages they're sending out are downright dangerous! Bring back innocence, bring back imagination, bring back quality storytelling. Bring back British children's TV! Show your support by joining the campaign Save Kids' TV: *www.savekidstv.org.uk*

Best wishes
Dean Wilkinson

FOREWORD
By Ant McPartlin

Be warned, be very warned: Dean's Classic Children's TV Quiz Book is going to cause you a whole load of brain-aching, memory-scraping, hair-pulling moments. You may very well find yourself angrily pacing the house for hours as the answer to a question like - which actor played Fred Mumford in the first series of Rentaghost – is on the tip of your tongue! However, you may, like me, be pushed over the edge when some annoying git rings you up and gives you the answer before it comes to you! What were the chances of that?!

And even if you don't recall some of the many many programmes mentioned in the book, there's still a boat load of facts and figures about the children's telly of days gone by that'll keep riveted for hours upon end. This is nostalgia at it's best, so get comfortably seated on your Raleigh Chopper, open a can of Top Deck, a packet of Spangles, and dip into The Children's TV Quiz Book and discover just how misspent your youth was.

Ant McPartlin

FOREWORD
By Dec Donnelly

Cheers, Dean, The Classic Children's TV Quiz Book has opened up a new social chapter of my life. I can now steer any conversation around to children's TV and rattle off fascinating fact after fact I've gleaned from this tome of tots, toddlers and teenage telly testimony, impressing anyone within earshot.

For example, I rang Ant and said, 'Morning Anthony, not to be confused with the late Anthony Jackson who played Fred Mumford in the first series of Rentaghost in 1976.'

You see what I did, I flawlessly steered the conversation around to a subject I was knowledgeable in after having read the Rentaghost section of The Children's TV Quiz Book. I not only impressed my friend, I also imparted my learning to him. I put the icing on the cake when I sang the entire theme tune to Rentaghost to Ant and by the end of it he'd hung up – presumably overwhelmed with euphoric nostalgia for his youth. Indeed, the man Ant is now feverishly banging on my front door with a cricket bat in his hand. Bless, he wants to play in the park like the youthful carefree young scallywags we once were. Enjoy the book, I'm off to play out!

Dec Donnelly

For more information on the author, please visit:
www.deanwilkinson.co.uk

A PLETHORA O'PUPPETS

Children's telly has given us so many puppets over the years and they are a merchandising man's dream. *Pinky and Perky* for example *(they never married did they!)* Puppets are immortal, but their human animators and sidekicks are not and many tend to move on to more 'grown-up' telly before they get typecast.

Can you match the anthropomorphic characters with their one time, on screen human collaborators?

	PUPPET	HUMAN
1.	Nookie Bear	Chris Evans
2.	Gordon the Gopher	Andi Peters
3.	Lord Charles	Noel Edmonds
4.	Sooty	Roy North
5.	Orville the Duck	Roger De Courcey
6.	Lambchop	Ray Alan
7.	Posh Paws	Shari Lewis
8.	Zig and Zag	Mathew Corbett
9.	Ed the Duck	Phillip Schofield
10.	Basil Brush	Keith Harris

DID YOU KNOW?
Orville The Duck was named after Orville Wright who also *'wished he could fly'*. Mr Wright eventually did.

AUTHOR'S NOTE:
Neil Waters stole my Gordon The Gopher puppet from me and tried to throw up in it because I'd been annoying him with it. That's him named and shamed *(we were both 23 at the time by the way)*.

RENTAGHOST

If you wanted to hire a ghost in the 70s and 80s, you rang Rent-A-Ghost, an agency of spooks, run by spooks. Fast paced schoolboy wit and some of the greatest character actors - sadly many of them really are ghosts now. Michael Stainforth (1942 – 1987) was the glue that held the show together.

11. Name the mischievous poltergeist jester - Edward Tudorpole or Timothy Claypole?

12. Which actress played Hazel The McWitch - Molly Weir or Phyllida Law?

13. Anthony Jackson played the ghost who started the agency, but was the character's name Peter Geist or Fred Mumford?

14. Name the long suffering neighbours of the Rentaghost crew - the Perkins, Jenkins or Larkins?

15. What was the troublesome pantomime horse called - Dobbin, Trigger or Winnie?

16. Can you remember the first line of the theme song? (Hint: it mentions a mansion house.)

17. In which year did the show begin - 1970, 1973, 1976 or 1979?

18. What year did the show end - 1984, 1986, 1989 or 1993?

19. Which human character did the late actor Edward Brayshaw play - Harold or Bertram Meaker?

20. In which soap did Sue Nicholls (Nadia Popov) later 'pop up'?

DID YOU KNOW?
Prime Suspect writer Lynda La Plante played the part of Tamara Novek.
Ann Emery, who played Ethel Meaker, is the sister of the late comedy genius Dick Emery - egad, Mistress Meaker, 'tis true!
Anthony Jackson, the actor who played the ghost who started the agency, sadly died in 2006, like Stainforth he was a truly gifted actor and we salute them both.

SWAP SHOP

Swap Shop was a ground breaking Saturday morning format as it was the first show to rely heavily on live phone-ins and outside broadcasts. Viewers could ring in and swap their old crap with a complete stranger's old crap. Enigmatic Noel Edmonds was the shopkeeper with the nicest beard on telly.

21. What was the show's full title?

22. Was Cheggers' outside broadcast feature called Keith's Klutter Klearout or Swaporama?

23. How many episodes did it run for - 99, 146, 172 or 209?

24. Which children's newsreader was also a presenter?

25. Was the never-seen technician who lowered the prize globe every week called Pat, Dave or Eric?

26. How did the dinosaur puppet Posh Paws get his name?

27. In which year did *Swap Shop* finally close its doors - 1980, 1981 or 1982?

28. Name the spoof pop group Edmonds, Chegwin and Philbin were in - Ketchup, Piccalilli or Brown Sauce.

29. And what was the name of their single?

30. Presenters Keith Chegwin and Maggie Philbin are brother and sister, true or false?

DID YOU KNOW?
Cheggers' outside broadcasts were usually filmed at sports grounds where the BBC had cameras already set up to film that day's sporting event to save money.
There were four Swap Shop annuals released during the course of the show containing features such as knitting patterns – oh how times have changed! Presenter Noel Ernest Edmonds is an accomplished helicopter pilot and played the helicopter mad schoolboy Harry Copter in the show, often interviewed by Noel via split screen pre-record.

THE MUPPET SHOW

(1976 to 1981) Set in an old style music hall, The Muppet Show featured a dazzling array of hilarious puppets as they tried to put on the best entertainment show they could. It was an instant success and creator Jim Henson's company went on to produce a long line of TV specials and Muppet movies.

31. **Which two characters had a tempestuous, long term love affair?**

32. **Name the *Star Trek* spoof sketch featuring a crew made up of pigs.**

33. **In what kind of hospital was a recurring sketch set?**

34. **Were the heckling old men in the balcony Waldorf and Salad or Waldorf and Statler?**

35. **What nationality was the chef?**

36. **Was the useless stand up comic bear called Fonzie, Floozie or Fozzie?**

37. **Dr Bunsen Honeydew had a long suffering lab assistant - was he Beaker, Petri or Scope?**

38. **How many episodes were produced - 60, 120, 200 or 420?**

39. **What was the name of the colossal, fierce looking seven foot tall Muppet monster - Cuddles, Luvbug or Sweetums?**

40. **John Denver, John Wayne and Johnny Cash – which one *didn't* appear on the show?**

DID YOU KNOW?
Creator Jim Henson (1936 – 1990) was unable to get the show off the ground in America, then ATV in England offered to make it.
Jim died of organ failure after feeling ill but not wanting to bother a hospital.
Puppeteer and voice artist Frank Oz did many of the Muppet characters before going on to do Yoda in the Star Wars films.

COSGROVE HALL

Brian Cosgrove and Mark Hall founded the Cosgrove Hall animation company in 1976 and have produced a vast array of successful and wonderful kids' cartoons and stop frame animation shows. Still going strong, Cosgrove Hall's productions are the benchmark of quality and imaginative formats.

41. Name the boy who had a Magic Torch - Johnny, Jules or Jamie?

42. Which *cushty* comedy actor voiced Count Duckula?

43. In which famous show did Cockleshell Bay first begin?

44. Which of Roald Dahl's books did Cosgrove Hall turn into a film?

45. Who voiced Engie Benjy (2002) - Dick and Dom, or Ant and Dec?

46. Which 1950's iconic puppet show did Cosgrove Hall remake in 2002 - *Rag, Tag* and *Bobtail* or *Andy Pandy*?

47. In 2003 Cosgrove Hall animated the *Dr Who* webcast *Scream of the Shalka*. Who played the Doctor - Richard E. Grant or Derek Jacobi?

48. Which *Good Life* star voiced *Alias the Jester*?

49. Was their 1987 show about a group of bugs and insects called *Creepy Crawlies* or *Quit Bugging Us*?

50. Which cartoon in the Kenny Everett Video Show did Cosgrove Hall animate - *Gitfinger in the Black Hole*, or *Captain Kremmen*?

DID YOU KNOW?
Chorlton and *The Wheelies* is banned in Israel because in one episode, a Star of David appears on a spell book instead of what should have been a pentagram, and because the book had a German accent it was deemed offensive.
In 2006 Cosgrove Hall animated lost episodes of the 1968 Dr Who adventure *The Invasion*. The company also animated the spooky, gothic webcasts of *Ghosts of Albion* (2003).

WHOSE VOICE IS THAT? (1)

It's hard to imagine many of the greatest kids' animations being so successful without the finest actors and actresses lending their familiar voices to the shows. Or what if the producers had got it wrong and, for example, never asked the legendary Peter Sallis to work on *Wallace and Gromit* and got some one trick pony like Samuel L. Jackson to do it? *'Hey dawg, these are the wrong, mother ******* pants.'* It just doesn't bear thinking about.

Try and match these wonderful shows with the voices that helped make them great.

51.	*The Trapdoor* (1984)	**Griff Rhys Jones**
52.	*Mary, Mungo and Midge* (1969)	**John Alderton**
53.	*Bod* (1975)	**Arthur Lowe**
54.	*Funny Bones* (1992)	**Richard Baker**
55.	*The Wind In the Willows* (1984)	**Neil Morrissey**
56.	*Bob the Builder* (1999)	**Ron Moody**
57.	*The Mr Men* (1975)	**John Le Mesurier**
58.	*The Animals of Farthing Wood* (1992)	Neil Innes
59.	*Raggy Dolls* (1987)	**Willie Rushton**
60.	*Fireman Sam* (1985)	**Ian Carmichael**

DID YOU KNOW?
Kids today aren't completely robbed of charismatic, memorable voices in their animation shows. *Andy Pandy* returned in 2004 voiced by Tom Conti, and *Bill and Ben* came back in 2005 with Jon Thomson voicing. There have been a lot of new shows too, notably the charming *Gordon The Garden Gnome* with the rustically recognisable Alan Titchmarsh providing voices.

HAPPY DAYS

Created by Garry Marshall, *Happy Days* was an instant hit all over the world. Showing the comical side of life in 1950s' America, it introduced us to the super cool Arthur (*The Fonz*) Fonzarelli. How much do you remember about it though, will you get a super cool Fonzie thumbs up, or can you go (and) *'sit on it'*?

61. Which rock'n'roll song was used as the theme tune for series one and two?

62. Who played the Fonz - Harry Cockler or Henry Winkler?

63. What was the Fonz's one word catchphrase?

64. *Happy Days* was set in New York - true or false?

65. What part did film director Ron Howard play in the series?

66. Name the redheaded practical joker played by actor Donny Most - was it Rufus Doofus or Ralph Malph?

67. Which 1970s' leather clad rock chick played the feisty Leather Tuscadero?

68. Which drive-in and burger joint did the characters meet at?

69. What year did the show start -1969, 1972, 1974 or 1976?

70. And can you remember the year it finished -1980, 1984, 1988 or 1990?

DID YOU KNOW?
Anson Williams, (who played Potsie) has a second cousin called Henry Heimlich who invented the famous, life-saving, Heimlich Manoeuvre.
Anson is now a successful director and has directed episodes of *Star Trek Voyager*, *Sabrina the Teenage Witch* and *Charmed*.
Ron Howard has directed such colossal box office movie successes as *Splash*, *Cocoon*, *Apollo 13* and *The Da Vinci Code*.

HAPPY DAYS SPIN OFF SHOWS

Happy Days was crammed with so many loveable and fantastic characters, it was inevitable they would spill out into other shows. Not only did *Happy Days* give us several spin off series, it gave us the phrase '*Jumping The Shark*', which refers to when a show runs out of ideas and adopts unbelievable characters and ludicrous storylines. Like the episode where Fonzie water-skis over a live shark. Not cool. See if you can remember the spin-offs.

71.　　Name the show featuring the two beer factory girls?

72.　　In the opening sequence, what does one of the girls put on a beer bottle?

73.　　Were their two loser, biker boy neighbours Larry and Squawky or Lenny and Squiggy?

74.　　Who played the alien Mork who visited *Happy Days* then got his own show?

75.　　What planet was Mork from - Dork, Ork or New Tork?

76.　　What was Mork's spaceship shaped like - a sausage, an egg or a croissant?

77.　　Can you remember Mork's catchphrase, said whilst bending his ears?

78.　　Name Mork's unseen boss to whom he had to report each week - Carson or Orson?

79.　　Joanie Cunnigham got her own series too, along with boyfriend Chachi, what was it called?

80.　　Name the animated version of *Happy Days*, made by Hanna-Barbera.

DID YOU KNOW?
Debatably, there were two other shows that were spin-offs from the *Happy Days* stable. They were *Blansky's Beauties* (1979) about Las Vegas showgirls, and *Out Of The Blue* (1977) about an angel in training, living with a normal family. Neither had any strong links to the original show *Happy Days* and lasted only one season each. They never aired in the UK, presumably because they were one shark-jump too many for the more discerning Brits.

THE GHOSTS OF MOTLEY HALL

Five earthbound spirits trapped in a tumbledown stately mansion just trying to get along and kill some time. This classic comedy from 1976 was an absolute delight that can still hold its own against any modern day TV show. The fantastically watchable Freddie Jones played the long dead, incompetent General who was the self imposed leader of the spooks. Available on DVD, you really must get hold of a copy.

81. Was the General called Sir Arthur Gasbag or Sir George Uproar?

82. Which *Last of the Summer Wine* actor played the long suffering estate agent trying to sell the hall?

83. Was the estate agent called - Mr Gherkin, Graplin or Gudgin?

84. Bodkin the professional fool was played by which superb **English** actor? Note I've highlighted the word English.

85. Bodkin died after getting a cold because he was repeatedly thrown into what - a duck pond or a barrel of Malmsey Wine?

86. How many series were there of *The Ghosts of Motley Hall* - one, three, five or seven?

87. Did Shelia Steafel play the mysterious White Lady, Grey Lady or Pink Lady?

88. Name the drunken, duelling ghost - Sir Francis, Sir Cumference or Sir Alan?

89. Name the stable boy who could actually go outside the hall - Jim or Matt?

90. The last owner of Motley Hall died when something knelt on him, was it a horse or an elephant?

DID YOU KNOW?
In the episode *Old Gory*, the late character actor Gerald James (1917 – 2006) played a ghost hunter called Mr Porter. Gerald also played a ghost hunter in *Sapphire and Steel* called Tully in Assignment 2.
Shelia Steafel was once married to *Steptoe and Son* star Harry H. Corbett.
The Ghosts of Motley Hall was another triumph for the genius writer Richard 'Catweazle' Carpenter.

ANIMAL SHOWS: PAWS AND EFFECT

There have been a menagerie of children's television shows about animals, factual and fictional. Some have gone on to be faithful old family pets that need a good fussing every time they're broadcast, whilst others have had to be taken out into the barn and quietly put to sleep with a commissioning editor's shotgun. So which ones do you remember? Have you got the memory of an elephant or a goldfish?

91.   Which TV legend presented the long running *Animal Magic*?

92.   Name the 1966 African based show featuring Clarence the cross eyed lion?

93.   Which 1966 series featured a heroic kangaroo?

94.   Name the Aussie presenter of *Animal Hospital* (1994 – 2004).

95.   In *Gentle Ben* (1967 – 1969), what kind of animal was Ben?

96.   From 1993 to 2006, which show did Michaela Strachan present?

97.   Name the 1989 CITV show which was about a boy who turned into a dog.

98.   What breed of dog was Lassie?

99.   Which 1959 show used live rodents voiced by human actors?

100.   Name the 1975 show about a milkshake and classical music loving frog and his orchestra?

DID YOU KNOW?
The theme to *The Adventures of Black Beauty* (1972 – 1974) is actually called Galloping Home and was composed by Denis King who also wrote the themes to *Dick Turpin*, *Worzel Gummidge* and *Just William*.
Before she was famous Michaela Strachan worked as a kissogram and an Avon lady, presumably not at the same time.

DIFF'RENT STROKES

When his employee passes away, the wealthy and kindly Mr Drummond adopts her two African-American sons. Being poor and coming from Harlem they find it hard adjusting to a life of money and security – with hilarious results. This show is a good example of one that doesn't quite stand the test of time. It's cheesy, sentimental and all American, but you have to remember, it was tackling some rather weighty issues of the time, so it's worth a second look.

101. Name the diminutive actor who played Arnold Jackson.

102. Can you recall his famous catchphrase?

103. Who was the elder brother, Arnold or Willis?

104. The family had a maid - true or false?

105. Was Mr Drummond's first name Phillip, Henry or George?

106. In which American city did the family live - San Francisco or New York?

107. What year did the show begin - 1972, 1978, 1981 or 1985?

108. In what year was it cancelled - 1986, 1989, 1990 or 1992?

109. Which famous pop star played Willis's girlfriend in the show?

110. Complete the saying 'Diff'rent strokes for --- '

DID YOU KNOW?
Dana Plato played Kimberly Drummond. Plato's career went into a nosedive after the show and she even took roles in seedy sex films (*what you talking about, willies?*) She died from a drug overdose in 1999.
Todd Bridges who played Willis is a former cocaine addict and was acquitted of the murder of a drugs dealer in 1988. In 1997 he was acquitted of attempted murder following a separate incident. Nice lad.

HANNA-BARBERA

Animation directors William Hanna and Joseph Barbera teamed up to create one of the most influential and prolific animation companies of all time. Okay, they weren't the most cinematic or complex animations, but they were certainly some of the most enjoable. Here are some quickfire questions about those glorious toons.

Can you remember which show was about...

111.   A kung-fu crime fighting dog?

112.   A family of sophisticated Neanderthals and their neighbours?

113.   Thieving, tie wearing bears living in Jellystone Park?

114.   A community of little blue people with white hats?

115.   A gang of New York alley cats?

116.   Three fun loving, whacked-out, hippy bears?

117.   A mystery solving all girl pop band?

118.   A dune buggy and its drivers solving mysteries in between races?

119.   A thawed out caveman nutter and the crime solving Teen Angels?

120.   A laid back, blue dog with a Southern American accent?

DID YOU KNOW?
Hanna-Barbera also did cartoon versions of *Laurel and Hardy*, *The Addams Family*, *Happy Days* and *Mork and Mindy*.
There was a short lived Hanna-Barbera Land theme park in Texas (1984 – 1985). It featured a Scooby Doo rollercoaster and a Papa Smurf restaurant. You may also recall the Hanna-Barbera shows *Quick Draw McGraw*, *Godzilla* and *The Harlem Globetotters*. More recent shows include *The Powerpuff Girls*.

FINGERBOBS

Presented by the actor Rick Jones, *Fingerbobs* was a very basic show about the various finger puppet animals that Rick brought vividly to life. Fingermouse was the main puppet, a crafty wonder-mouse that could swerve past cats. How much do you recall about this imaginative, laid back little gem?

121. *Fingerbobs* was originally shown as part of what other show?

122. In what year did Fingerbobs begin - 1960, 1965, 1972 or 1977?

123. In the show was Rick Jones' character was called Nerf, Papa or Yoffy?

124. Rick presented on another classic BBC pre-school show, name it.

125. Exactly 100 episodes were made - true or false?

126. Was the ping-pong ball headed seagull character Gulliver or Guinevere?

127. There was a tortoise finger puppet too. Was he called Zoom or Flash?

128. Is Rick Jones Australian, Canadian or French?

129. Was the aquatic, redheaded Fingerbob called Lobster or Scampi?

130. From the theme music, complete the line 'These hands are made for making and making they --- '

DID YOU KNOW?
Rick Jones allegedly destroyed Fingermouse with the cameras still rolling when the series ended.
Rick's folk band was called Meal Ticket and their song *Better Believe It Babe* was used as the theme for the 1980 BBC Play For Today 'The Flipside Of Dominic Hide'.
Fingermouse, minus his human operator, got his own show on BBC1 in 1985, but only lasted one series.

I DON'T REMEMBER THAT! (1)

There have been an abundance of long forgotten quality TV shows that didn't quite rise to the top. See if you can recall some of these 'well worth remembering' gems.

Which show ...

131.   Featured a small American town that was the centre of weirdness? It had a marauding Bigfoot, a tornado hunter and dogs wanting to take over the world. American TV 1991 – 1992.

132.   Was a time travelling romp about two kids who slipped into the past and future via a time barrier? It ran for four series but was, uniquely, classed as one 26 episode production. ITV 1970-1971.

133.   Featured Hartley Hare, Madam Octavia and Topov the monkey? Pig had a thick Brummie accent and loved cream buns. It was originally set in a puppet workshop. ITV 1973 – 1981.

134.   Was a Swiss stop-frame clay animation piece about penguins, focussing on one in particular? There was no dialogue save for a garbled kind of honking. BBC 1986, remade 2004.

135.   Was set in Middlesbrough and was about a young boy, his dog Razzle and his rough, but likeable family? It had a theme tune performed by a brass band. BBC1 1985.

136.   A black and white, 1960s, Yugoslavian series about a girl and her friendship with her Uncle's horses? It was shown in the seventies during summer holidays, dubbed into English. RTS Yugoslavia/BR-TV Germany 1965.

137. Ran from 1973 to 1980 and contained one ex-Goons star, a myriad of tiny, crazy little puppets, and a lot of potty goings-on? ITV.

138. Was a puppet show set in a seaside town where ghosts come out at night to help the friendly Sidney Sludge in his dealings with his wicked sister Sybil? ITV 1993 – 1995.

139. Featured a child like king in constant need of reassurance and advice? He had a wise cat called Hamlet. This was basic animation and was voiced by Ray Brooks. BBC 1980.

140. Was a lunchtime sing-a-long 10 minute filler that lasted 379 episodes? The presenters would literally sit there and sing you songs, even taking requests from the public.* ITV 1978.

(*Although they didn't even reply to a letter in 1980 from a 13 year old boy in Thornaby-on-Tees asking them to perform a rendition of The Stranglers' classic No More Heroes. They'd have ruined it anyway!)

DOCTOR WHO –
THE CLASSIC SERIES

If you're old enough, you can – they say – remember exactly where you were the day Doctor Who started on 23rd November 1963. Sat in front of the telly presumably. Shame the bloke who shot Kennedy on that same day* hadn't been watching the first incarnation of the renegade time travelling hero then, hey? He'd have saved a whole heap of trouble. And mess.

141. **From which planet does the Doctor hail from?**

142. **Was the Doctor's vintage yellow car called Old Girl or Bessie?**

143. **Which actor played the very first Doctor, Jon Pertwee or William Hartnell?**

144. **Two of the Who actors share the same surname, what is it?**

145. **The original series ended in 1989, but what number Doctor did Sylvester McCoy play?**

146. **What military organisation was the Doctor scientific advisor of?**

147. **The Brigadier's full name was Alistair Gordon Lethbridge-Stewart - true or false?**

148. **Name the Doctor's arch-enemy, a renegade fellow Time Lord.**

149. **Which evil aliens set the Loch Ness monster on London - Daleks or Zygons?**

150. **Which evil aliens could be killed by gold dust - Sontarans or Cybermen?**

DID YOU KNOW?
Doctor Who is the longest running television sci-fi show in the world.
In the 1976 adventure The Brain Of Morbius, past and future incarnations of the Doctor are shown, one of which was production assistant Graeme Harper who is now a director on the new series.
Peter Cushing played a human Dr Who in two 1960s' film versions of the show, Doctor Who and the Daleks (1965) and Daleks – Invasion Earth 2150 AD which also starred Bernard Cribbens who returned to the show in 2007 as Wilfred Mott.
*That's 'same day' if you could travel by TARZIBAS, which stands for Time And Relative Zones In British And American Space.

MAID MARIAN AND HER MERRY MEN

Created by, and starring, all round entertainer and lovely chap Tony Robinson, *Maid Marian* was an instant hit with both children and adults. It lampooned the Robin Hood legend reducing Robin's character to a vain, incompetent fool with Marian as the real hero. It was a constantly surprising and refreshing show containing wry social commentary, surreal anachronistic concepts and spontaneous musical numbers.

151. What wicked bad-guy part did Tony Robinson play?

152. Did the wonderful actor Danny John-Jules play Harrington or Barrington?

153. In this show was Robin Hood's profession a banker or tailor?

154. Who was the King's wet-behind-the-ears nephew from Gisbourne?

155. Was the very big, strong and stupid merry man Little Tom or Little Ron?

156. The short, angry and violent one was called Rabies - true or false?

157. Were the King's friendly, yet dim, guards Norris and Neil, or Gary and Graeme?

158. Can you remember the cruel and hated King's name?

159. In what year did the show begin on BBC1 - 1975, 1980 or 1989?

160. How many series of Maid Marian were there - two, four, six or eight?

DID YOU KNOW?
Tony appeared in the 1975 film *Brannigan* which starred the late John Wayne.
Tony also lent his voice to the CITV show *Nellie The Elephant* (1989 – 1991).
Danny John-Jules, who was Cat in *Red Dwarf*, also played Milton Wordsworth in the Cbeebies show *Story Makers*.

THOMAS THE TANK ENGINE

Made by The Britt Allcroft Company, *Thomas The Tank Engine* has received international acclaim for its amazing models and sets. Boasting one of the catchiest TV theme tunes ever, what was not to like about the reliable little train and his friends – and these were the only British trains that seemed to run on time with none of the toilets blocked up with bog paper and stale urine.

161.   Is Thomas a blue or a green engine?

162.   On what fictional island does Thomas work - Sodor or Kudos?

163.   Thomas's human boss, Sir Topham Hatt, is nicknamed what?

164.   The original books were written by Bishop T.K. Wilma - true or false?

165.   Is Thomas described as '*A really clever train*' or '*A really useful engine*'?

166.   Did Ringo Starr narrate the show from 1984 – 1990, or 1989 – 1999?

167.   The show was later voiced by actor Michael Angelis - true or false?

168.   What number is on Thomas's side - 1, 5, 7, or 9?

169.   Not one of Thomas's fellow engines - Irving, James or Henry?

170.   In what year was the first Thomas book printed - 1895 or 1945?

DID YOU KNOW?
Thomas's design is based on the 1913 steam locomotive E2 class 0-6-0, and if you find that interesting then you're a git.
Of Ringo Starr, John Lennon was once asked if Ringo was the best drummer in the world, to which he replied, '*I don't even think he was the best drummer in the Beatles.*'

GAMESHOWS – WIN SOME TAT

Long ago it was enough for a kid to get his or her face on the telly. They'd be the talk of the school for months, so this presumably is why most of the prizes they used to offer on children's gameshows were quite naff. Offer 21st century kids a Crackerjack pencil and they'd ask you to turn it on for them, or stick it in you. It's hard to imagine any of the formats in the shows below being relevant today. Apparently Sky One is developing the kids' gameshows Win Booze *and* Fags for you and Your Social Worker *and* Double Your ASBOs.

Which show ...

171.   First aired in 1969, and was a panel show where teams of kids were tested on film clips? It also featured the Young Film Maker of the Year Award and was largely hosted by Michael Rodd. Brian Trueman and Mark Curry took over respectively until its demise in 1984. BBC.

172.   Was hosted by the ever charming, larger than life Christopher Biggins with the leopard skin clad, saucy score-girl Gillian Taylforth (later of EastEnders)? It was set in the jungle and ran from 1982 – 1985. It had a great catchphrase too! ITV.

173.   Boasted the legendary comedian and actor Mike Reid (1940 – 2007) as its host who was more than a little rough with the kiddy contestants? There was lots of shouting and confusing rules and it ran from 1975 – 1981. Stan Boardman and Leslie Crowther tried presenting it, but were just too nice so Reid returned. ITV.

174.   Was a zany, gunge and games romp hosted by the (n)ever popular Pat Sharp sporting THE worst mullet ever? His two cohorts were sexy cheerleading twins Melanie and Martina Grant. The craziness culminated in the rip-roaring one m.p.h. go cart race at the end. 1989 ITV.

175.   Followed a pop music based format hosted by the

always brilliant and well loved Keith Chegwin? Two schools would compete in pop based games and quizzes and a top chart group of the day would play 'live.' It started in 1978 before it was 'Ta-ra' in 1986. BBC.

176. Was set on the faraway planet of Arg where visiting Earth celebrities were tested in logic and mathematical problem solving? It featured Moira Stewart, who was in fact a shape changing alien dragon, and featured special effects that were cheap even in the 1980s. 1980 – 1986 BBC.

177. Featured two students against one who picked letters from a board and answered questions beginning with that letter? There was also Goldruns and a host so smooth he could have been (*and was on radio!*) James Bond. 1983 – 1993 ITV.

178. Was perhaps not technically a kids' show, but was a massive hit with them? It was a series of bizarre tasks, in different styled zones, given to a bunch of young people, firstly by a Rocky Horror baldy, then by another English eccentric who was a direct descendent of Henry VIII. 1990 – 1995 Channel 4.

179. Was again, in essence, not exactly a children's show but you had to either be a kid or bloody stupid to enjoy it? Teams competed in the most ridiculous of costumes doing bungee runs and ascending greased poles. Host Stuart Hall famously nearly passed out with laughter nearly every episode. 1966 – 1987 BBC.

180. Was a groundbreaking 1980s' game show, featuring competing children in a computer generated, early virtual reality, medieval fantasy setting? Kid contestants had to wear the *Helmet of Justice* (mainly because they couldn't have seen the blue screen effects anyway). Hosted by Treguard. 1987 – 1994 ITV.

BLUE PETER

Match the famous *Blue Peter* presenters with the year they STARTED on the show. Tricky, yes, but recalling memorable moments from this wholesome family magazine show might help you pair faces with years. And no, not the elephant poo incident – sheesh, grow up.

181.	Valerie Singleton	1987
182.	Anthea Turner	1967
183.	John Noakes	1983
184.	Matt Baker	1962
185.	Caron Keating	1958
186.	Peter Purves	1992
187.	Janet Ellis	1986
188.	Christopher Trace	1989
189.	John Leslie	1965
190.	Yvette Fielding	1999

DID YOU KNOW?
A Blue Peter is a maritime flag, hoisted by ships in ports that are ready to sail.
Monty Python's catchphrase 'And now for something completely different' was stolen from *Blue Peter*.
The original presenter Christopher Trace played the body double for Charlton Heston in *Ben-Hur* (1959). He was sacked from *Blue Peter* in 1967 for having an affair with a hotel receptionist. Trace died in 1992.
The famous theme tune to the show is called Barnacle Bill.

BLUE PETER APPEALS

Remember when Blue Peter appeals were exciting? We'd tune into B.P. twice a week just to see how high the scoreboard had climbed and talk about it the next day at school. Were they really such innocent times, or were we just really boring kids? Whatever the reason the Blue Peter appeals have done some damn fine things over the years and long may they continue. See if you can match the items collected with the appeals.

191.	1964 Silver paper	For an old people's bus
192.	1965 Wool	For children's hearing aids
193.	1966 Old books	For a tractor for Uganda
194.	1969 Toy cars	For baby unit apparatus
195.	1970 Spoons and forks	For water purification equipment in Java
196.	1971 Pillowcases and socks	For guide dogs
197.	1972 Scrap metal	For a Kenyan boys' dormitory
198.	1981 Used stamps	For three caravans for under privileged kids
199.	1985 Old keys	For the Lifeboat Association
200.	1989 Old tin cans	For an old people's centre

DID YOU KNOW?
The most innocuous presenter was arguably Simon Groom, but old Groomy had a wicked sense of humour and would often ad-lib sexual innuendo into the live show, much to the chagrin of legendary editor Biddy Baxter.
Presenter Michael Sundin, a former gymnast, was fired in 1985 after being caught up in a gay sex controversy, although the official reason was because he was crap. He died of AIDS in 1989.

TIMMY MALLETT

The son of a vicar, Timmy Mallett has delighted radio and telly audiences of all ages with his random, slapstick and friendly schoolyard wit. With a never ending battery of energy and a dress sense based on, what can only be described as 'Dali kicking off in a cake shop', Timmy is one of the rare English eccentrics who can actually pull off 'zany', be funny, and remain cool. He's in an elite group populated by the likes of Harry Hill, Spike Milligan and The Pythons.

201. What was Timmy's 1984 Saturday morning show called?

202. Name the 1985 spin off show.

203. Timmy's game, in which he physically hit people, was called Brain Bosh or Mallett's Mallet?

204. Was Timmy's cockatiel called Magic, Muffins or Monster Mash?

205. Which *groovy* Canadian actor got his first break on Timmy's show?

206. Is the 2007 Five kid's show Timmy voices on called Roary *The Racing Car* or *The Beeps*?

207. Is Timmy's catchphrase Amazingly Awesome! or Utterly Brilliant!?

208. What was Timmy's pop band called? Bomwacaday, Bombularina or Bombleurgh?

209. And what was their number one single called?

210. Was Timmy's 1997 CITV panto style series *Timmy Turrets* or *Timmy Towers*?

DID YOU KNOW?
Timmy's stuffed mallet is called Pinky Punky and is famous for peeing on the audience at live gigs and pantos. He also once hit Margaret Thatcher over the head with it.
Timmy is a connoisseur of fine art and an acclaimed painter. His work can be seen at www.brillianttv.co.uk

STUPID

Set in the mythical Ether World, this sketch show/sitcom reveals that a pan-dimensional race of God-like entities – Deed Monarchs - rule over all of mankind's behaviour. King Angry makes people short tempered, whilst Queen Sensible promotes level-headed behaviour. The show's focus is King Stupid who controls all of the stupidity on Earth.

211. Which two comedians have played the part of King Stupid?

212. Which female Deed Monarch does King Stupid secretly fancy?

213. What kind of creature is Goober the butler - a boggart or a gremlin?

214. Is Goober orange with a purple suit or purple with an orange suit?

215. Which bit of Goober ignites if a human sees him - his nose or tail?

216. Complete Gobber's famous nickname 'Bog House ---'

217. If a Deed Monarch appears in the mortal world do they change into a chest of drawers or a tree?

218. How does the Deed Monarch King Wonderful make humans feel?

219. What's the catchphrase of the boy who pokes people with his bedevilled finger?

220. In one series of sketches, what does Graham's Gran keep pretending to be, just to annoy him?

DID YOU KNOW?
Rusty Goffe, who played the part of Goober, was one of the Oompa-loompas in the 1971 film *Willy Wonka* and *The Chocolate Factory*. Rusty also played a Jawa in the 1977 film *Star Wars* as well as being the famous bouncing weatherman from the defunct cable channel *Live TV*. Rusty is indisputable proof that the best things come in small packages and we salute you Mr Goffe!

PLAY SCHOOL

'Ready to knock, turn the lock, it's Play School', the iconic, educational, make and do, use-your-imagination show devised by Joy Whitby which ran from 1964 to 1988. We all watched this show long after we'd become too old for it simply because it was brill! Here are some questions about our favourite pre-school show, *ready to play?*

221. Was the rocking horse called Dappledown or just Dapple?

222. Jemima was the show's real life cockatoo - true or false?

223. Which famous English actor, surprisingly, presented the show?

224. Give the surnames of presenters Floella, Chloe and Brian.

225. Was presenter Toni Arthur male or female?

226. What were the two teddy bears called?

227. Which egg shaped toy kept falling over on screen?

228. What was the show's sister programme aimed at older kids?

229. Name the three shaped windows viewers had to guess we would look out of?

230. Which 21st century pre-school show uses the same device - *Tikkabilla* or *Doodle Do*?

DID YOU KNOW?
Play School was the first programme to be shown on BBC2 because a power failure prevented the previous night's adult viewing.
Hamble the doll was despised by all the presenters and was often drop kicked around the studio, off screen of course. Presenter Fred Harris also fronted *Ragtime* (1973) and *Chock-A-Block* (1989).

I DON'T REMEMBER THAT! (2)

Another collection of ne'r repeated children's shows for you to screw your face up at and say *'Must've been before my time.'*

Which show ...

231. Was another stop animation classic from Ivor Wood and FilmFair and revolved around some hats living together in the same town? Each hat's character was stereotypical of what it represented. Sancho the sombrero was Mexican, for example. BBC 1969.

232. Brought the world of variety to a young audience and ran from 1969 to 1974? Singers, dancers, comedians, even hated jugglers got to showcase their talents, or lack of it in the case of bastard jugglers. Bobbie Bennett presented, Jess Yates produced. ITV.

233. Featured puppets in a medieval castle where Queen Ethelbruda and King Woebegone lived? There was oil under the castle so they were constantly under siege from the Hasbeenes. ITV 1977.

234. Was a collection of weird short films from around the world and had THE most haunting theme tune? It was largely presented by Alan Rothwell, or *'that bloke with the one sticky out ear'*. ITV 1969 –1990.

235. Was a pre-school puppet show set in the house where Humphrey Cushion lived with Dusty Mop and, occasionally, Alan Rothwell? ITV 1973.

236. Was a make and do show hosted by post-*Magpie* Susan Stranks and two spiders called Itsy and Bitsy? ITV 1974.

237. Revolved around a magical panda that fell off the back of a lorry? His name was taken from 'This Side Up, Use No Hooks' printed on his crate. ITV 1977.

238. Had an egg shaped gemstone character who lived in a wood and enjoyed playing the music of Mozart? BBC 1977.

239. Was a non-verbal cartoon about a frizzy haired girl and her dog having fun? It also featured Birdie and Butterfly. BBC 1972.

240. Starred a brave horse as it's central character in America's wild west? There was also a dog called Rebel. CBS 1955.

GRANGE HILL (1)

Like most people have their own Doctor Who, many have their own favourite set of characters from Grange Hill. Right from the start it courted controversy and dealt with sometimes dark, gritty storylines. In its day it was must-see-TV! Millions of kids rushed home to watch the goings on in a modern comprehensive school, usually after a day in a modern comprehensive school of their own. The phrase 'Busman's holiday' meant little to kids back then.

241.   Which prolific TV writer created *Grange Hill*, and later *Brookside* and *Hollyoaks*?

242.   In what year did the show start -1974, 1976 or 1978?

243.   In the original comic-strip titles what is thrown on the end of a fork?

244.   In which English city was it originally set?

245.   Which actor played the scary Mr Bronson - Michael Sheard or Michael Ripper?

246.   Name the 1986 anti-drugs song connected to the show?

247.   Which character became a heroin addict, Tucker, Zammo or Gripper?

248.   Whose car did Danny Kendall die in - Mrs McClusky's or Mr Bronson's?

249.   Which famous model appeared once as a non-speaking extra in 1982?

250.   Can you remember the spin-off series about Tucker Jenkins?

DID YOU KNOW?
The original Grange Hill theme was called Chicken Man and was written by Alan Hawkshaw. Bizarrely, it was used as the theme tune to Give us a Clue at the same time. Hawkshaw also composed the Countdown jingle played as the clock ticks away the 30 seconds thinking time.

GRANGE HILL (2)
TEACHER FEATURE

Like real teachers, the many Grange Hill tutors were of varying degrees of likeability. Many superb actors portrayed these long suffering educationalists, some so brilliantly you almost smell the coffee breath coming out of your telly.

See if you can match the Grange Hill teacher with the lessons they taught.

	TEACHER	SUBJECT
251.	Mr Sutcliffe	Art
252.	Mr 'Bullet' Baxter	Music
253.	Miss Moony	Computers
254.	Mr 'Scruffy' McGuffy	Science
255.	Miss Booth	Drama
256.	Mr Bronson	Nothing: Was Head Teacher
257.	Mr 'Hoppy' Hopwood	English
258.	Mr Hankin	P.E.
259.	Mrs McClusky	Woodwork
260.	Miss 'Sexy' Lexington	French

DID YOU KNOW?
Actress Paula Ann Bland, who played schoolgirl Claire Scott, shocked the nation when she got her *Grange Hills* out (appeared topless) in Mayfair in 1988.
Michael Cronin, who played Mr Baxter, is also a successful children's author. His first novel was *Against The Day* and is set in a Nazi occupied England.
Michael '*Mr Bronson*' Sheard sadly passed away in 2005, he was a superb actor who starred in many brilliant TV shows and films. We salute you Michael!

GRANGE HILL (3) WORKS EXPERIENCE PLACEMENTS

Once an actor's name becomes synonymous with a hit show it is sometimes hard for them to move on without being typecast to that role. Particularly for child actors, and many often fade back into obscurity – the words **Rol** and **And** spring to mind. Some get away with it though.

Match the famous former Grange Hill stars with another big show they've become linked with.

	ACTOR	TV SHOW
261.	Kim Hartman	Press Gang
262.	Claire Buckfield	E.R.
263.	John Alford	Bottom
264.	Brian Capron	EastEnders
265.	Susan Tully	The Bill
266.	Terri Dwyer	Allo Allo
267.	Todd Carty	London's Burning
268.	Lee Cornes	Coronation Street
269.	Alex Kingston	Hollyoaks
270.	Mmoloki Chrystie	2.4 Children

DID YOU KNOW?
Former *Grange Hill* (and *Holby City*) actress Laura Sadler died when she fell from an upstairs room in 2003 in London. Her character in the show - Judi Jeffries - also died from falling out of an upstairs room four years earlier.
Alison Bettles, who played Fay Lucas (1982 – 1987) has returned to acting after rearing a large family of four children. Her son Albert Valentine played the spooky, gas mask wearing Jamie in *The Empty Child* and *The Doctor Dances*, part of the 2005 series of *Doctor Who*.

SPACED OUT

Kids' shows set in outer space have always been an easily identifiable and reusable format, but they haven't always been a sure-fire rocket ride to stellar success. Here's some you might need a Tardis to go back and reacquaint yourself with.

Which show ...

271. Was about a motley crew of veterinary misfits who flew about the cosmos helping sick creatures? There was a talking dog called Dogsbody too. Top comedy actress Anne Bryson starred. BBC 1992.

272. Followed the everyday life of a futuristic, out of this world, family who had robots, hover-cars and all manner of techno-wizardry at their command? The dad still complained about working three hours, three days a week. American TV 1962.

273. Was a sitcom created by *Rentaghost's* Bob Block and was set inside a spaceship being chased by space pirates and robots? The dazzling Kenneth Williams (1926 – 1988) provided the voice of the snooty computer S.I.D. BBC 1985.

274. Was about an ex-N.Y.P.D. cop who is transferred to the rough Demeter City Police Station on the planet Altor? With his partner Haldane they investigated crimes made by and against aliens. Sky 1994.

275. Featured a know-it-all robot dog who was a former side kick of a certain space and time dwelling hero? Intended as a spin off from that hero's own show, it only ever made it to pilot. Elisabeth Sladen starred. It has possibly THE worst theme tune ever. BBC 1981.

276.   Was about the Foxwoods, a family of astro-farmers on a remote asteroid in space? Splodger and Biff from the asteroid Gorpdale kept trying to steal the farm's produce. ITV 1992.

277.   Was also set in space, the final frontier, showed us the cartoon adventures of the crew of a famous spaceship as it looked for new alien life (but not as we know it)? BBC 1973.

278.   Was a cartoon based on Greek mythology? After killing the Giant Cyclops, a space captain is damned to roam the cosmos with his frozen crew. He had his son Telemachus and the small robot Nono for company. BBC 1981.

279.   Was made by Gerry Anderson and featured an elite task force who defended Earth against alien attacks from the likes of the evil Zelda? There was also the tough Sergeant Major Zero, a robot Spheroid, voiced by the wonderful Windsor Davies. ITV 1983.

280.   Was originally a Japanese cartoon about five young heroes of G-Force? Mark, Jason, Princess, Tiny and Keyop who battled the evil Zoltar from Spectra using their amazing, transforming ship The Phoenix. BBC 1978.

DOCTOR WHO (2) – THE CLASSIC SERIES

Monsters and villains. There's been a veritable carnival of monsters since the time travelling Time Lord opened the doors to his Type 40 in 1963. But how many of these evil, wicked and downright punchable rogues can you match with their home planet. To make things easier, three of the buggers come from the same 'hood'.

VILLAIN	HOME PLANET
281. The Master	Sontar
282. Giant Spiders	Gallifrey
283. Daleks	Mondas (Telos is acceptable)
284. The Time Meddler	Mars
285. Cybermen	Gallifrey
286. Sontarans	Metebelis 3
287. Giant Robot	Mechanus
288. Ice Warriors	Gallifrey
289. Mechanoids	Earth
290. The Rani	Skaro

DID YOU KNOW?
Planet of the Spiders wasn't the original planned finale to Jon Pertwee's swan song in 1974. A story called *The Final Game* was written which would see The Master revealed as the dark side of the Doctor's personality. The Master would then be killed off actually saving The Doctor. The story was never written, however, because the actor Roger Delgado, who played the Master so wonderfully, sadly died in a car accident in Turkey. The loss of his good friend drove Jon Pertwee to hand over the role to Tom Baker. The Doctor's dark side was revealed as The Valeyard in Colin Baker's story *Trail Of A Timelord*.

WACKY RACES

Another smash hit cartoon for Hanna-Barbera, Wacky Races featured many weird and wonderful characters competing in different long distance races. Road rage has never been so much fun, but can you match the demented driver(s) to their crazy cars?

DRIVER(S)	CAR NAMES
291. Dick Dastardly and Muttley	The Creepy Coupe
292. Peter Perfect	The Army Surplus Special
293. The Ant Hill Mob	The Crimson Haybailer
294. Professor Pat Pending	The Mean Machine
295. Sergeant Blast and Private Meekly	The Boulder Mobile
296. The Slag Brothers	The Turbo Terrific
297. Lazy Luke and Blubber Bear	The Compact Pussycat
298. Red Max	The Convert-a-Car
299. The Gruesome Twosome	The Arkansas Chuggabug
300. Penelope Pitstop	The Bulletproof Bomb

DID YOU KNOW?
Only 17 episodes were ever made. There were two spin off shows, *The Perils of Penelope Pitstop* (1969) and *Dastardly and Muttley in their Flying Machines* (1969) which is often wrongly remembered as *Catch The Pigeon*. Ventriloquist Paul Winchell originally voiced Dick Dastardly, but he also invented and patented the first artificial heart – bizarrely! He sadly died in 2005.

PRESS GANG

Set around a children's newspaper, *Press Gang* was a sophisticated comedy drama that ran for five dazzling series written by the amazingly gifted Steven Moffat. The scripts were so beautifully crafted it could easily slip from laugh-out-loud comedy to serious issues such as child abuse, glue sniffing and suicide. *Press Gang* is the benchmark for perfect kids' telly.

301. Name the children's newspaper - *The Norbridge Enquirer* or *The Junior Gazette*?

302. Which actress played the stroppy editor Lynda Day?

303. Was the first long suffering deputy editor - Kenny or Tony Phillips?

304. Who was the loveable, wide-boy, entrepreneur in charge of accounts - Andy or Colin Matthews?

305. Dexter Fletcher played Spike, but was his surname Thomas or Thompson?

306. Which 'nutty boy' pop star guest starred in the episode *Friends Like These*?

307. Was Lynda's, often put upon, kindly English teacher Mr Sullivan or Mr Roe?

308. How many episodes were made - 33, 43, 53 or 63?

309. In what year did the series begin -1982, 1986, 1989 or 1994?

310. What was the last ever episode called - *They Might be Giants* or *There are Crocodiles*?

DID YOU KNOW?
The orignal idea was by Moffat's father Bill and was called *The Norbridge Files*.
Bill wrote four novels based on *Press Gang*.
Steven Moffat has written some fantastic episodes for the new Doctor Who including *The Empty Child*, *Blink* and *Silence in the Library* and took over the role of executive producer from Russel T. Davies in 2008.

WORZEL GUMMIDGE

This 1979 show about a greedy, mischievous scarecrow was based on the books by Barbara Euphan Todd and starred the late, great Jon Pertwee (1919 – 1996). Also featuring the very cream of British characters actors such as Una Stubbs, Geoffrey Bayldon, Joan Sims, Michael Ripper and Mike Berry, it couldn't fail to delight both young and old. The first time Worzel had been brought to life on screen was in 1953 with *Worzel Turns Detective* starring Frank Atkinson (*a four part BBC series*), but it's Pertwee's series that takes the turnip.

311. Which farm was Worzel supposed to be guarding crops for - Farmer Giles' Farm or Scatterbrook Farm?

312. Name the field where Worzel worked - Two Acre Meadow or Ten Acre Field?

313. Who was the mysterious creator of Worzel and all the other scarecrows -The Strawman, The Turnipman, or The Crowman?

314. What bit of his body did Worzel change when it suited him?

315. Can you remember Worzel's favourite snack, and catchphrase?

316. Played by the wonderful Una Stubbs, who was Worzel's true love?

317. Which bubbly *Carry On* film star played the part of Saucy Nancy?

318. What was Saucy Nancy, a shop dummy or a sailing ship's figure head?

319. Lorraine Chase played another of Worzel's fancy women, was she Dolly Clothes Peg or Sophie Sparkle?

320. Were the last two series relocated to Australia or New Zealand?

DID YOU KNOW?
There were six series of *Worzel Gummidge* in total and featured cameos from Bernard Cribbins, Billy Connelly and Bill Maynard. In series one it was uncovered that Worzel's middle name was Hedgerow.
Una Stubbs is also an accomplished artist and has had exhibitions of her work.
The actress Charlotte Coleman, who played the little girl Sue (series one to four), went on the star in *Four Weddings and a Funeral*. Charlotte sadly died from an asthma attack in 2001. She was 33.

I DON'T REMEMBER THAT! (3)

Another collection of kid's shows that were shown while you were out playing.

Which show ...

321. Was a cartoon about a boy who could breathe underwater by eating special chewing gum called Oxygum, and his dolphin friend called Splasher? BBC 1969.

322. Revolved around a cartoon flying ark filled with two headed creatures one of which was happy, the other grumpy? Richard Briers did voice work. BBC 1976.

323. Was about a stage magician called Tarot who also had very real supernatural powers and solved mysteries with his young chums, and an owl named Ozymandias? ITV 1970.

324. Featured a stop animated bear who wanted to sing and dance and travel the world? The superb Colin Jeavons narrated this - originally French - show. BBC 1973.

325. Was a cartoon about fruity superhero Eric Twinge who lived at 29, Acacia Road? It was voiced by *The Goodies*. BBC 1983 – 1986.

326. Featured an animated band of noble dogs and was based on The Three Musketeers. Originally produced by the fantastic Spanish animation company B.R.B., it was re-dubbed into English. ITV 1981.

327. Was the animated, everyday life of a family of fur balls? The children were called Perkin, Posie and Pootle. BBC 1976.

328. Was a simple animation show, narrated by John Le Mesurier, about a bald headed boy? Other characters included Aunt Flo and PC Copper. BBC 1975.

329. Followed the adventures of Robin and Rosie Cockle in their seaside town where their parents ran The Bucket and Spade Guest House? Began as part of *Rainbow*. ITV 1980 - 1986.

330. Brought swine fever to Britain insomuch the nation fell in love with the puppet presenters with the squeaky voices? They were identical, but one wore blue and one wore red – which didn't much help on black and white telly! Numerous appearances and shows from 1957 to present, just name the characters.

GERRY ANDERSON – HEROES

Responsible for some of the finest, and highly regarded, children's shows of all time, Gerry Anderson pioneered puppet and live action filming techniques, as well as model making standards, that remain breathtaking even by today's standards.

Can you place the heroes in their correct shows?

	SHOW	HERO
331.	Space 1999	Scott Tracy
332.	Stingray	Harry Rule
333.	Space Precinct	Joe McClaine
334.	Thunderbirds	Mike Mercury
335.	Fireball XL5	Ed Straker
336.	U.F.O.	Patrick Brogan
337.	Terrahawks	Commander Koenig
338.	Joe 90	Dr Tiger
		Ninestein
339.	The Protectors	Steve Zodiac
340.	Supercar	Troy Tempest

DID YOU KNOW?
Gerry's puppet shows were filmed in Supermarionation, which is the system he developed of using marionettes suspended by wires that both supported and controlled the figures. Some wires also controlled mouth and eye movements inside the puppets' heads. As this technique was honed the puppets heads became smaller and thus, more lifelike. Compare the bulbous head sizes of the Thunderbirds' puppets to the head sizes in *Captain Scarlet*.

WILLO THE WISP

First hitting our screens in 1981 on BBC1, *Willo The Wisp* was a magical, animated journey into a surreal and unforgettable world introduced by the welcoming Willo, a ghostly being made of gaseous, blue light. It was first shown on weekdays just before the 6 o'clock news so we watched it putting our shoes and coats on before going out. Magical.

341. Which multi-gifted comedy actor voiced all the parts in the show?

342. In what wood did the series take place - Crivens or Doyley?

343. Evil Edna the witch was a walking, talking........what?

344. With what did she zap her victims?

345. Was the overweight, inept, but sweet fairy Mildred Crete or Mavis Cruet?

346. What was the dog called - Robert, The Moog or Little Phatty?

347. Name the rather stuck up, Noel Coward-esque cat - Carwash or Waxunpolish?

348. What type of creature was Arthur - a frog or a caterpillar?

349. Before being turned into The Beast, was he a prince or a milkman?

350. Can you remember what the little yellow bird was called - Twit or Nugget?

DID YOU KNOW?
Willo The Wisp was originally created by Nick Spargo for a series of adverts by British Gas. There were 26 episodes made, each being five minutes long. A second series of *Willo The Wisp* was made in 2005 and voiced by *My Hero* actor James Dreyfus. This series saw Evil Edna becoming widescreen, with a wheeled base, and hundreds more channels.

THE KRANKIES

Many so-called satirical types have tried to sum up what The Krankies are in derogatory ways. All you really need to know is they are is nothing short of brilliant. Inventive, madcap, hilarious and superbly entertaining, the Krankies first appeared on our screens in 1973 on *The Wheeltappers and Shunters* and went from strength to strength. Wee Jimmy Krankie is the cheeky scamp of a schoolboy and the stuffy grown up foil is Ian. Fantastic chemistry and wonderful comic timing, The Krankies we salute you!

351. What is Jimmy Krankie's real name? (*you do know it's a woman!*)

352. In real life are they brother and sister or husband and wife?

353. Coincidentally, what year were they both born - 1947, 1953 or 1960?

354. Which long running BBC kids' show did they co-present in 1981-82?

355. Was their ITV 1983-85 show *The Krankies Klub* or *Krankies at Large*?

356. You MUST remember Jimmy's catchphrase?

357. Was their *Krankie's Elektronik Komik* (1986-87) for ITV or BBC?

358. Is Jimmy's school cap green, blue or red?

359. Was their ITV 1987-91 show called *Krankies TV* or *Krank Up D'Krankies*?

360. In 1981 they released a single, named after their catchphrase, but how did it fare? Did it reach number 1, 46, or 146?

DID YOU KNOW?
In 2003 Wee Jimmy Krankie was voted The Most Scottish Person In The World by The Glasgow Herald.
In 2004 she was badly injured during a fall whilst performing in Jack and The Beanstalk. Thankfully she made a full recovery.
The Krankies appeared in a sketch on Channel 4's 1997 *Ant & Dec Unzipped* with Alistair McGowan called *Och Jock, I'm The New Doc* – penned by the author of this book!

RAINBOW

Often parodied, but never bettered, *Rainbow* is one of the most fondly remembered British TV shows and over 1,000 episodes were made in the original run. They tried to bring the show back in 1996 entitled *Rainbow Days*, but without the wonderful Geoffrey at the helm the magic wasn't there anymore.

So what do you remember about the classic series?

361. What was the first line of the theme song?

362. Was Geoffrey's surname Hambly, Hayes or Hayden?

363. Before *Rainbow*, Geoffrey played DC Scatliff in which vintage BBC cop show - *Softly Softly* or *Z-Cars*?

364. Who presented the show before Geoffrey - David Nixon or David Cook?

365. Voice artist Roy Skelton did the voice for Zippy, George *and* Bungle - true or false?

366. Was George a boy or a girl?

367. What did Rod, Jane and Freddy do together once an episode?

368. The original series ran from 1970-1989, 1972-1992, or 1976-1995?

369. *Rainbow* was ITV's answer to which American pre-school show?

370. In the very early episodes, were the two main glove puppets Nelly Night and Dotty Day, or Sunshine and Moony?

DID YOU KNOW?
Before Rod, Jane and Freddy, there was Rod, Matt and Jane. Matt was actually Matthew Corbett in his pre-Sooty and Sweep days.
Several actors played Bungle over the years including John Leeson who was also the voice of K9 in *Doctor Who*.
Roy Skelton also voiced the Daleks in the classic series of *Doctor Who*.

MAGIC MOMENTS

Long before Harry Potter minced onto his first broomstick (*oh come on, you're a young boy wizard and all you do is levitate feathers when you could be conjuring up naked ladies and bottles of cider!*), there was a host of wonderful and wacky witches and wizards on children's TV. How many can you remember?

Which show ...

371. Had a young girl with an over active imagination who was the only one in the village of Little Hemlock who could see a witch? BBC1 1973 - 1975.

372. Starred the comic genius Stanley Baxter as a bumbling alien wizard sent to Earth for constantly failing his wizarding exams and ending up a supply teacher – poor sod? ITV 1988 - 1990.

373. Was about a wicked tea drinking witch, hell-bent on world domination who kept kidnapping a small boy called T-Shirt? Elizabeth Estensen starred. ITV 1985 – 1992.

374. Featured Mildred Hubble, a young witch who constantly finds herself in trouble at witch academy? The always wonderful Una Stubbs starred as Miss Bat. ITV 1998.

375. Was a six part adventure in which young Kay Harker is entrusted with a magical box by a strange old man he meets at a railway station? Second Doctor Who Patrick Troughton starred. BBC 1984.

376. Was an American show about a teenage girl who just wants an ordinary life despite enjoying the fruits of being a witch and living with her two witchy, yet downright foxy, aunts? ITV 1996 – 2000.

377. Ran on BBC1 and starred Ron Moody. It was about two sorcerers, the good Rothgo and the bad Belor who fought over the powerful Nidus? 1980 – 1982.

378. Developed from the shows of Rod Hull and Emu and centred around a wicked green witch and the strange characters she lived with, Croc and Robot Redford? ITV 1991 – 1993.

379. Boasted pre-*EastEnders* stars Adam Woodyatt and Anna Wing? When an English church is moved it throws up a whole heap of trouble such as ghosts, timeslips and witchcraft before an ancient stone - the Grinnygog - can be found by three eccentric, kindly old witches. BBC 1983.

380. Had a lad called Simon who makes friends with an over inquisitive, but well meaning, witch who leads him into embarrassing and tricky situations? BBC 1987.

SCOOBY DOO (1)

Another Hanna-Barbera smash hit classic cartoon which has stood the test of time. But what can you remember about the golden years of Scooby and co? And if these questions are too easy then 'We'd have gotten away with it if it wasn't for your pesky good memories!'

381. What name do the ghost hunting gang go by?

382. Can you remember the name of their van - The Mystery Machine or The Spook Sedan?

383. What type of dog is Scooby-Doo?

384. Which character's real name is Norville Rogers - Fred or Shaggy?

385. What's Daphne's second name - Blake, Baker or Brook?

386. The bespectacled, brainy girl is Thelma Dinkle - true or false?

387. And what is she famous for losing in the show?

388. Name the food the gang use to bribe Scooby to do things.

389. Which of these is not a Scooby-Doo catchphrase - Zoinks!, Willies!, Jinkies!

390. American DJ Stacy Kasem originally voiced Shaggy - true or false?

DID YOU KNOW?
At the concept stage, the show was originally called *Mysteries Five* and the characters were all members of a rock group who solved mysteries between gigs. The band members were Geoff, Kelly, Mike, Linda, W.W. and their dog Too Much. According to legend the name Scooby Doo comes from the ad lib by Frank *Ol' Shut Eyes* Sinatra at the end of his tuneless rendition of *Strangers in the Night*.

SCOOBY DOO (2)

Many are the tales told of the legendary, ghost-fearing, junk food chomping, detective mutt Scoobert Doo, Scooby for short. Over the years he's appeared in many different shows, compendium shows, specials, and live action films. So can you match the Scooby Doo cartoon shows, and one off TV films, with the years they first aired?

391.	*Scooby Doo Where Are You?*	*1983*
392.	*The New Scooby-Doo Movies*	*1987*
393.	*The Scooby- Doo Show*	*2002*
394.	*Scooby-Doo And Scrappy-Doo*	*1985*
395.	*The All New Scooby-Doo and*	
	Scrappy-Do Show	*1972*
396.	*The 13 Ghosts Of Scooby-Do*	*1976*
397.	*Scooby-Doo Meets The Ghoul Brothers*	*1989*
398.	*A Pup Named Scooby-Doo*	*1969*
399.	*Scooby-Doo and The Reluctant Werewolf*	*1979*
400.	*What's New Scooby-Doo?*	*1988*

DID YOU KNOW?
In 1996 The Fun Lovin' Criminals released the single Scooby Snacks. In the song, Scooby Snacks are actually diazepam tablets the banks robbers take to control their nerves. Nice!
We've also met many of Scooby's family over the years, such as Scooby Dum, Yabba Doo, and his parents Momsie and Dada Doo. Oh, and that little turd Scrappy Doo.

SPACE 1999

A nuclear explosion blasts the Moon out of Earth's orbit and sends it soaring through the galaxy. The crew of the Moonbase are left lost, alone and searching for a new home on an adventure that brings them into contact with all manner of strange alien life forms, some good, some bad. Actually, mostly bad. Stinkers some of 'em. This was Gerry Anderson's second science fiction, live action epic, the first being *UFO*, and was equal to its predecessor in terms of gripping storylines and astounding visual effects.

401. Was the name of the Moonbase – Centuri - Phoenix or Alpha?

402. Who played Commander John Koenig - Martin Landau or Ed Bishop?

403. What were the fleets of spacecraft called - Beagles or Eagles?

404. Who played Helen Russell - Barbara Baine or Shelley Winters.

405. Who played the shape changing alien Maya - Catherine Schell or Gabrielle Drake?

406. What planet was Maya from - Muton, Psychon or Rutan?

407. Was the head pilot called David, Alan, Chris or Tom Carter?

408. Barry Morse played Professor Victor Bergman - true or false?

409. How many episodes were made - 38, 48, 58 or 68?

410. Award yourself innumerate points if you can remember the exact day the Moon left orbit.

DID YOU KNOW?
Space 1999 attracted many huge names as guest stars including Peter Cushing, Christopher Lee, Joan Collins, Brian Blessed, Leo McKern and Patrick Troughton.
An episode of the American show *Wonder Woman*, entitled *Time Bomb*, used footage of the Moonbase cut from Space 1999.

THE CLANGERS

The year *The Clangers* debuted, the space race between the Americans and the Russians was reaching its peak. The British played their part by sending two heroic men to a barn in Whitstable, Kent – armed with a shoe-string budget - to create this highly imaginative science fiction classic. The rest is history, but can you remember any of it?

411.   In what year did the show begin - 1964, 1969 or 1973?

412.   Oliver ----? created and narrated *The Clangers*.

413.   Were the Clanger puppets made of tin foil, wool or plasticine?

414.   Was the Clangers' staple diet String Theory Stew or Blue String Pudding?

415.   Name the broth producing dragon who lived under the planet's surface.

416.   Were the small, orange characters with black, spindly legs - Owlets or Froglets?

417.   Did the Clangers communicate by static, beeps or whistles?

418.   Which character lived in an orbiting nest - the Tinfoil Turkey or the Iron Chicken?

419.   Name the gaseous character that floated around making music - The Ion Storm or The Cloud?

420.   How many episodes were made in total - 13, 27, 39 or 42?

DID YOU KNOW?
In the 1972 Doctor Who adventure *The Sea Devils*, an incarcerated Master passes his time watching *The Clangers*. This was parodied in the 2007 Who episode *The Sound of Drums* when John Simm's Master was seen watching *Teletubbies*.
In the 1967 Noggin The Nog book, *Noggin and the Moon Mouse*, a Clanger like alien mouse falls to Earth. First contact?

SPONGEBOB SQUARE PANTS

Imagine the audacity of pitching an idea like SpongeBob Squarepants. An animated cartoon, set under the sea, and the central character is naive to the point of idiocy. Oh, and he's a talking sponge who works in a burger joint. Someone must have been listening because it's simply one of the finest cartoons ever produced. A future vintage classic. See how much you know about SpongeBob and co. Are you ready kids? I can't heeeeaaar you.....etc, etc.

421. In which town is the show set - Bikini Bottom or Beachbum Boomtown?

422. What type of fruit is his house made out of - a strawberry, an orange or a pineapple?

423. Where does Bob work as a fry cook - Neptune's Burger-Sea-King or The Krusty Krab?

424. Bob's mean boss is called Mr Luke Sidewalker - true or false?

425. Is Bob's grumpy, clarinet playing neighbour Squidward or Squidgerald?

426. Who is Bob's non-too-bright friend - Patrick Jelly or Patrick Star?

427. SpongeBob's pet snail is called Barry, Harry or Gary?

428. Is the air breathing squirrel that sometimes calls on Bob called Sandy Rea or Sandy Cheeks?

429. Who is the tiny, power crazy owner of the Chum Bucket - Silas Shrimp or Mr Plankton?

430. Is the live action pirate who introduces special editions called Long John Underwear or Patchy the Pirate?

DID YOU KNOW?
SpongeBob is the brainchild of animator Stephen Hillenburg who also happens to be a marine biologist and drew his inspiration from that. The original character was called Sponge Boy.
Veteran actor and American legend Ernest Borgnine occasionally lends his voice to the show as Mermaid Man - the actor is well remembered for his other underwater role as Detective Rogo in the *Poseidon Adventure* (1972.)

I DON'T REMEMBER THAT! (4)

More shows you missed because they were obscured behind that shaft of sunlight on the screen which kids today don't know anything about because of all this flat-screen mumbo-jumbo.

Which show ...

431.   Was a sitcom set in a burger bar in Cricklewood run by two squabbling, but secretly in love, Canadians, one of which was played by the wonderful Jennifer Calvert? *ITV 1990 – 1992.*

432.   Was adapted from a Helen Cresswell novel about a spoilt child who can see ghosts that turn out to be Victorian kids asking for help through time? Almost exactly the same story as *The Amazing Mr Blunden*. *BBC 1988.*

433.   Began as a series of stories written by HRH The Duchess Of York, Sarah Fergusson, about a brave little helicopter? It became a cartoon series running from *1993 – 1996 on ITV.*

434.   Was about a rather dim-witted alien called Angelo who comes to Earth via a wardrobe in a boy called Mike's bedroom? It was, allegedly, a comedy. *ITV 1989 – 2000.*

435.   Revolved around the antics of a furry, wisecracking, cynical, cat eating alien life form secretly living with a normal suburban family called the Tanners? *American TV 1986 – 1990.*

436. Was a drama set in a kids' hospital ward and was quite hard hitting for children's telly, dealing with subjects like paedophilia, cancer and drink and drugs problems? Russell T. Davies wrote and produced some of it. ITV 1995 – 1998.

437. Featured an American school teacher who chances upon the fountain of youth, takes a sip, then infrequently becomes a 12 year old boy – often at the most embarrassing of times? American TV, but aired on BBC 1976 – 1977.

438. Centred around a large foster family? A gritty drama with humour and charm, and with the brilliant Lee Ross starring as Dodger it couldn't fail to please. ITV 1985 – 1987.

439. Ran as part of the *Watch With Mother* slot? It was a gentle, puppetry show about a family who lived on a farm with their dog Spotty. Daddy never wore a shirt and the acting was a bit wooden. BBC 1955.

440. Was another Jim Henson smash hit about an amazing underground world populated by many different species of creatures, all dependent on one another? Comedy legend Fulton Mackay (1922-1987) was the only human in the British version. ITV 1983 – 1987.

CAPTAIN PUGWASH

Hey ho, me hearties! The most useless pirate on the sea, but you couldn't help but love him. Captain Pugwash was unique as it was a cartoon filmed in real time. The backgrounds were stage sets and the characters were cardboard cut-outs with moveable mouths so they could be synchronised to the pre-recorded voice track. Amazing stuff.

441. Can you remember Pugwash's first name, was it Ahab, Horatio or Nelson?

442. Was Captain Pugwash's ship called The Black Pig or The White Elephant?

443. Was the dopey, malapropism spouting, second in command named 444, Mister Mate or Master Mate?

444. The cabin boy was called Roger - true of false?

445. Was Pugwash's enemy called Shiver-Me-Timbers Tony or Cut-Throat Jake?

446. Name this bad pirate's ship - The Flying Dustman or The Leaky Barrel?

447. In what year did the first episode air - 1957, 1967 or 1977?

448. How many episodes of the original TV series were made - 13, 45 or 86?

449. Have a shiny doubloon if you know who voiced all the characters.

450. Have a treasure chest if you know the real name of the theme tune.

TONY HART

Few things can evoke such delightfully warm hearted, goggle-box-watching memories as the name Tony Hart. This breathtakingly gifted, gentle voiced artist and presenter brought us thousands of hours of awe inspiring art show telly. He also made wearing a cravat look effortless and sported a white mane of hair so slick it could have been crafted by Michelangelo. Quintessential Englishman Tony Hart, we salute you, sir!

451. On which programme for deaf children did Tony appear during 1964 to 1977?

452. In this show, was the viewer's art section called Hanging's Too Good For 'Em or The Gallery?

453. Can you remember the first of Tony's own art shows 1978 – 1984 - was it *Hart Luck* or *Take Hart*?

454. In this show, who was the bungling caretaker who interrupted Tony - Mr Bennett or Mr Bus?

455. Name Tony's 1985 -1994 show? (*It sounds like a Yorkshire Police show set in the 1960s.*)

456. Who was Tony's speechless little plasticine chum - Moschops, Maurice or Morph?

457. Which famous TV badge did Tony design?

458. In the 1960's show *Titch* and *Quackers*, which one of the two puppets did Tony operate?

459. In which year was Tony born - 1895, 1915, 1925 or 1935?

460. Tony made his TV debut on which Saturday morning show - *Saturday Splatterday* or *Saturday Special*?

DID YOU KNOW?
Before Tony broke into television, when he was short of cash he painted murals in restaurants in exchange for meals.
In WW2, Tony was an officer in the Ghurkhas.
He has a daughter called Carolyn and two grandchildren.
And do you remember the fantastic, eccentric, Yorkshire, handlebar moustache wearing inventor who appeared with Tony from time to time? Here's a clue, the answer is Wilf Lunn.

HERE COME *THE DOUBLE DECKERS*

Set in a junkyard and following the adventures of a gang of a well meaning kids, *Here Come The Double Deckers* hit our screens in 1971. Fast paced, visually stunning and downright funny, the show was an Anglo/American vehicle designed to be a modern day (by 1970s' standards) take on the 1950s' *The Little Rascals*. The forerunner of Double Deckers was a similar format called *The Magnificent Six And A Half*, which is less well remembered.

461. How many kids were there in the *Double Deckers* – six, seven, eight or nine?

462. In which English city was their junk yard situated?

463. Which versatile actor – and star of *Spooks* – played the leader Scooper, was it Paul Nicholas or Peter Firth?

464. Name the only American kid - Stripes, Stars or Sticks.

465. Was the posh, bespectacled clever-clogs Double Decker called Poindexter, Brains or Professor?

466. Debbie Russ played the youngest, soft toy hugging, kid, was she Teddy, Tiger or Tiny?

467. Played by Douglas Simmonds, who was the tubby, food loving character - Tubs, Piefast or Doughnut?

468. Gloria in *It Aint Half Hot Mum*, Albert in *Double Deckers*, name the actor – Melvyn Hayes or Don Estelle?

469. Brinsley Forde starred as which character - Pounce, Spring or Hyper?

470. How many episodes were made - 7, 17, 27 or 37?

DID YOU KNOW?
Only one of the child actors has made it as a successful adult thespian, although Gillian Bailey who played tomboy Billie, did play Ravella in the 1978 *Blake's 7* episode *The Way Back*, so that's something to tell the grandchildren.
After *Double Deckers*, Brinsley Ford turned his attention to music and formed the long running reggae group *Aswad* who had several hits in the 1980s.

BASIL BRUSH

The one and only true fox on the box has been a source of mirth since the early '60s and is still going strong with an ever growing army of loyal fans. Basil the puppet was created by legendary kids' TV stalwart Peter Firmin who also gave us *The Clangers*, *Noggin The Nog* and *Bagpuss*, to name but a few magical creations from his Smallfilms production company.

Originally appearing on *The Three Scampies* (1963) Basil shot to fame with his questionable wit, posh accent, and host of long suffering human foils such as Mr Derek, Mr Roy and Mr Billy. Like The Chucks and The Krankies, he's a mainstay of classic British children's telly and long may he live. Basil, you are a vulpine God and we salute you!

471. On which caddish, gap toothed English character actor is Basil based?

472. Which magician did Basil appear with in the '60s Paul Daniels or David Nixon?

473. Which *Likely Lads* star was once Basil's human foil?

474. Was Mr Derek's (Fowlds) tenure 1969 – 1973 or 1971 – 1972?

475. Was Mr Roy's (North) tenure 1973 – 1977 or 1975 – 1981?

476. Was Mr Billy's (Boyle) tenure 1977 – 1977 or 1979 – 1980?

477. *Let's Count With Basil Brush* or *Let's Read With Basil Brush*, his 1980s' educational show?

478. In 2005 which quiz show did Basil famously win for charity - *Are You Smarter Than a 10 year Old* or *The Weakest Link*?

479. Did Basil ever do a Jackass, crazy stunt Ch4 show called *Brush With Death*?

480. Which old Noel Edmonds show did Basil bring back in 2008 - *Telly Addicts*, *Swap Shop* or *Lucky Numbers*?

DID YOU KNOW?
Basil was originally voiced and operated by the reclusive Ivan Owen who refused to be pictured with the puppet in case it broke the illusion Basil was alive. Ivan sadly died in 2000.
Basil is the mascot of HMS Fox.
Because of his off the cuff remarks, Basil has been accused of racism and homophobia and was once investigated by the Northamptonshire Hate Crimes Unit – presumably his warm, downy brush proved too much of a soft target to resist, boom boom!

GET YOUR FACTS RIGHT!

Children's factual programmes also have their places in people's hearts – it's a fact! Get the right format with the right presenters and you're laughing all the way to the ratings bank. And, the crafty thing is, you can get kids to learn without them realising it! See which famous non-fiction classics you remember.

Which show ...

481.   Became many child's first contact with the news and current affairs? Hosted by everyone's chum John Craven, this wonderfully forward thinking idea was an instant hit and gave us all enquiring minds,.....for a few minutes! BBC 1972 – present day.

482.   Had the endearing Michael Aspel at the helm answering requests from the general public for clips from their favourite shows? Long before VCR, Sky Plus and You Tube, this was the only guaranteed way to see those clips again. BBC 1970 – 1981.

483.   Aimed to promote good reading with children and ran on ITV 1979 – 1989 and had a brilliant theme by Andrew Lloyd-Webber? Doctor Who originally presented it (the Tom Baker one) before the likes of Stephen Moore and Timmy Mallett took over.

484.   Was hosted by John Craven and was billed as the children's answer to *Mastermind*? It ran from 1974 – 1975 on BBC1 and had scoring 'computer system' called B.E.R.Y.L.

485.   Was a children's Film '72 because it showed clips of up and coming films, just like the ex-Barry Norman (and later Jonathon Ross) vehicle does now? This ran from 1972 – 1982. Hosted by the loveable Chris Kelly, ITV.

486. Was fronted by the impossible-not-to-love Johnny Ball who made maths and science fun? Yes, the bugger actually gave us after school learning and we never sussed him! Detention was never *this* good in this 1978 – 1984 unmissable show. BBC.

487. Featured record breaking attempts in virtually anything you could think of? It was hosted by the trumpet playing, tap dancing, comedy acting, television presenting Roy Castle (1932 – 1994). The show ran from 1972 – 2001, BBC.

488. Strove to answer all sorts of baffling science and history questions and puzzles that seemingly had no answer, ranging from rocket science to simple pub tricks? The legendary Fred Dinenage was at its core in all its incarnations, but the first run lasted from 1966 – 1981, ITV. Hands up.

489. Had possibly the longest title of any TV show ever, but was usually shortened to just three words? It aimed to promote boredom-breaking ideas for children, especially in school holidays. It was presented by kids from different areas, and ran from 1973 – 1995, BBC.

490. Made dreams come true for hundreds of kiddies, and all you had to do was write in and ask James Wilson Vincent Savile? He hosted the show throughout it's entire run 1975 – 1994, BBC. Now then, what was the show called? *Rattle rattle.*

CRACKERJACK (1)

Lumberjack? Steeplejack? Uncle Jack? Noooo, Crackerjack! The long running game, talent, sketch and music show had something for everyone and featured a myriad of wonderful entertainers in its 29 year run. Give yourself an extra point for every time somebody shouts out the word Crackerjack! whenever you say the show's title. Then punch the sod.

491. On what day did the show famously go out?

492. And at what famous time?

493. Was the original presenter of the show David Frost or Eamonn Andrews?

494. What was the perennial runners up prize?

495. What was Stu Francis's famous fruit destroying catchphrase?

496. The long running game where kids held arms full of prizes was called Double or Trouble - true or false?

497. What vegetable did kids have to hold if they got a question wrong?

498. Which game replaced this - Take a Bun or Take a Chance?

499. How many episodes were broadcast - 400, 750 or 1,000??

500. Which scruffy, cockney songsters penned [the later] Crackerjack theme - The Pet Shop Boys or Chas And Dave?

DID YOU KNOW?
Crackerjack was always broadcast live, but it was only in the 1970s did it go out at it's famous date and time.
In the 1980s its musical hall format was becoming a bit old hat and the show was scrapped.
Crackerjack attracted many big pop names in its time. The Who, The Small Faces and Status Quo are amongst the superstars who appeared.

CRACKERJACK (2)

Match the *Crackerjack* presenter with the years they presented the show. This is tricky and is more of a guessing game. To make it even more fun, for every correct answer award yourself a prize from your house, a toaster, a cushion or a small child for example – see how many you're left holding at the end. Ho ho!

	PRESENTER	YEARS PRESENTED
501.	Eamonn Andrews	1968 - 1974
502.	Peter Glaze	1955 - 1964
503.	Stu Francis	1964 - 1968
504.	Ed 'Stewpot' Stewart	1957 - 1960
505.	The Krankies	1973 - 1976
506.	Don Maclean	1980 - 1984
507.	Michael Aspel	1972 - 1972
508.	Leslie Crowther	1960 - 1979
509.	Little and Large	1975 - 1979
510.	Ronnie Corbett	1981 - 1982

DID YOU KNOW?
Crackerjack presenter Leslie Crowther went on to amazing success hosting *The Price is Right* and *Stars in their Eyes*. Sadly, his career faltered after a horrific car accident in 1992 which left him in a coma for 17 days and needing brain surgery. Leslie passed away in 1996 due to heart failure. He was an all round entertainer who brought charisma and class to everything he did, and we salute him!

BANANA SPLITS

(1968 – 1970) Tra la laa, tra la la laa! Who could forget that insanely catchy theme tune to *The Banana Splits Adventure Hour*. This was an absurd, blink-and-you-miss-it, high energy, magazine show featuring live action comedy, running gags and sketches, and animated shows. It's format was loosely based on Rowan and Martin's *Laugh-in* and was another big hit for Hanna-Barbera.

511.   The leader was Fleegle, but what kind of dog was he (clue – it rhymes with his name)?

512.   What kind of animal was Drooper - a rabbit, lion or a mouse?

513.   Drooper had an Agony Aunt section, was it called Dear Drooper or Drooper's Dilemmas?

514.   What kind of animal was Snorky - a rhinoceros or an elephant?

515.   What kind of animal was Bingo - a grinning Cheshire cat or a gorilla?

516.   Fleegle and Drooper played guitar, but what did Snorky and Bingo play?

517.   Who were the Splits' rival gang whom we never saw, The Animal Smackers or The Sour Grapes?

518.   How did they deliver messages to the Splits, by paper aeroplanes or non-stop dancing messenger girls?

519.   Name the cartoon D'Artagnan appeared in?

520.   How many episodes of *The Banana Splits* were made - 16, 25, 31 or 44?

DID YOU KNOW?
The Arabian Knights was another of the animated strands of the show. In it, the character Bez could transform himself into any animal and gave the world the catchphrase 'Size of a --' saying the name of the beast he would turn into. In 1991, pop group The Wonderstuff took inspiration from this for their classic hit *Size of a Cow*.

ROOBARB

This addictive little cartoon, about an overly adventurous and enthusiastic dog, first aired in 1974 and was an instant hit in the five minute slot just before the 6 o'clock News. The deliberately shaky animation, the brilliant characters, and the amazingly catchy theme tune all firmly secure *Roobarb* in the hearts and minds of anyone who's seen it. Every episode title started with the word 'when.' *When Custard Stole the Show*, or *When there was a Big Mix up*, for example.

521. What colour was Roobarb - purple, green or orange?

522. What kind of animal was the cynical Custard?

523. Can you remember what colour Custard was - pink, blue or grey?

524. Where would Roobarb usually invent things - the greenhouse or the shed?

525. Who sat in the trees watching all that went on in the garden - the birds or the squirrels?

526. Name the superb *Good Life* actor who narrated the series?

527. On which channel did *Roobarb* first air - BBC1 or ITV?

528. In the 1970s series, how many episodes were there - 20, 30 40 or 50?

529. Was the 21st century, second series called *Roobarb 21AD*, or *Roobarb and Custard too*?

530. Was the animator of Roobarb called Geoff Braintree or Bob Godfrey?

DID YOU KNOW?
The music was by Johnny Hawksworth who also wrote the theme tune to *George and Mildred*.
Roobarb was created by the gifted writer Grange Calveley who also gave us *Noah and Nelly in the Skylark*. Grange based the idea of *Roobarb* on his Welsh Border Collie who peed on his roobarb patch the first day he got the hound. Grange penned every episode of both series of the show. Grange, we salute you.

TISWAS

What can you say about the legendary Saturday morning show *Tiswas* that hasn't already been said – apart from it was a quiet, gentle and educational show. Of course it was none of these things. It was bloody bonkers and we loved it! It took a Saturday morning by the scruff of the neck, shoved a flan in its face and a bucket of water down its trousers!

531.   Who was the sexy female presenter of *Tiswas*?

532.   Was Chris Tarrant's famous catchphrase from the show – 'They had that coming!' or 'This is what they want'?

533.   Was Bob Carolgee's scruffy, gobbing, dog puppet called Spit or Phlegm?

534.   Who was the mysterious, masked, pie chucking character - The Phantom Flan Flinger or Captain Tart Tosser?

535.   Name Lenny Henry's newsreader character based on Trevor McDonald?

536.   Were the four piece pop group made up of presenters called *Pies in your Eyes* or *The four Bucketeers*?

537.   Can you remember the name of the record they had out - *Fling a Flan At Dan* or *The Bucket of Water Song*?

538.   What did T.I.S.W.A.S. stand for?

539.   David Rappaport played which dodgy character in the show - Reggies, Krazes, or Shades?

540.   How many episodes of *Tiswas* were made -165, 234, 302 or 452?

DID YOU KNOW?
Multi talented dwarf actor David Rappaport joined *Tiswas* in series eight (1981 – 1982). Unable to cope with depression, David tragically took his own life in 1990. He was just about to film the *Star Trek The Next Generation* episode *The Most Toys* and the part of Kivas Fajo had to be quickly recast with actor Saul Rubinek. We miss you David and salute you!

FROM SMALL SCREEN TO BIG SCREEN

Big movie moguls are constantly raiding the telly archives for something to turn into a blockbuster because they're downright lazy buggers. They want instant success so their movies must have an instant recognition factor. You wait, it won't be long before Johnny Depp stars in the big movie version of John Craven's Newsround. Bah! Anyway, these kids' TV shows were eventually made into films - true or false?

541.	*SpongeBob Square Pants*	True / False
542.	*The Double Deckers*	True / False
543.	*The Muppet Show*	True / False
544.	*Mr Benn*	True / False
545.	*Round The Twist*	True / False
546.	*Five Children And It*	True / False
547.	*The Monkees*	True / False
548.	*Rentaghost*	True / False
549.	*The Brady Bunch*	True / False
550.	*Rugrats*	True / False

DID YOU KNOW?
A big screen outing for a popular children's show can sometimes be as bad an idea as dissolving swimming trunks. In 2000 an Americanised film version of *Thomas the Tank Engine* appeared. *Thomas and The Magic Railroad* starred Alec Baldwin and was a massive flop. And do the *Narnia* blockbusters have any of the warmth and charm the BBC *Chronicles of Narnia* series had? No. They were fawn droppings by comparison.

SMTV LIVE

SMTV Live, or *Saturday Morning Television Live*, was an ITV magazine show that ran from 1998 to 2003, clocking up a rather splendid 279 episodes. Towards the end of its run it was hosted by several presenters including Tess Daly, Brian Dowling, H, Claire Richards, Steven Mulhern and Des Clarke, but its glory years are widely regarded as being when it was fronted by Ant, Dec and Cat. The onscreen chemistry between the three presenters was nothing short of electric and they provided us with some of the finest moments in the history of children's telly.

551. Name the sitcom that was always the last sketch on *SMTV Live* - Pals, Muckers or Chums?

552. What BBC Saturday morning show did SMTV trounce in the ratings, *Live and Kicking* or *Saturday Superstore*?

553. Was the obviously gay consumer rights superhero played by Ant Mr Dynamite Cycleshorts or Captain Justice?

554. Name the long running, weekly guessing game - Fool The Mule, Wonky Donkey or Ass The Family?

555. Cat played a younger, not as pretty, version of herself, was she Cat the Dog or Mogruff Deeley?

556. In what quiz did Ant pit his wits against children - Beat The Buffoon or Challenge Ant?

557. What section started with a mass dance to 'Please, Mr Postman', Letters and That or The Postbag?

558. What sketch was about glorious moments from Dec's life - Donnelly's Legacy or Dec Says?

559. Name the sketch which was a spoof of *Heartbeat*, with fart gags.

560. Name the hospital drama sketch, was it *Casually*, *Dolby City* or *Clean Sheets*?

DID YOU KNOW?
In the *Start Trek* spoof sketch *SMTV 2099*, Dec played the cowardly Captain D'Merde, a parody of the brave, French Captain Picard. Merde means excrement in French. In this sketch guest stars such as Victoria Beckham, were '*comically duped*' into drawing huge breasts on themselves on a see-through Perspex star map.
In the 2001 Channel 4 poll, *The 100 Greatest Kids' TV Shows*, SMTV Live came a very healthy number 27.

ANT AND DEC

Before they became a staple part of adult TV, bringing us shows like *Saturday Night Takeaway* and *I'm A Celebrity Get Me Out Of Here*, the Geordie presenters and actors Anthony McPartlin and Declan Donnelly cut their teeth on children's TV. Sometimes controversial, always exciting, they brought us many hours of appointment TV that will be long remembered – but by whom, you? Will you get the answers quickly? or is it a case of *let's get ready to fumble?*

561.   What was the very first show Ant presented in 1988 on BBC1, *Take Hart* or *Why Don't You?*

562.   In which Geordie kids' soap did they first act together as P.J. and Duncan?

563.   And in this show, who played Duncan - Ant or Dec?

564.   Whose character went blind - Ant's or Dec's

565.   How many series of their BBC1 *The Ant and Dec Show* ere there – two, four, six or eight?

566.   Which Monkees' song did the duo once cover - *Steppin' Stone* or *I'm A Believer?*

567.   Was Ant and Dec's only Channel 4 series called *Unravelled* or *Unzipped?*

568.   What pop show did they immediately present when *SMTV Live* finished?

569.   Which BBC show did they host where friends tried to win the holiday of a lifetime, *Ant and Dec's Getaway Gamble* or *Friends Like These?*

570.   As a rule, does Dec stand on the left of the screen, or the right?

DID YOU KNOW?
In *The Ant and Dec Show* (BBC1) there was an infamous quiz called 'Beat The Barber'. In it kids were placed in a barber's chair and asked questions with a view to winning prizes. If they lost, however, their hair would be totally shaved off. There was a national outcry about the idea despite the children involved saying it was the coolest thing to have ever happened to them.

STINGRAY

Yet another smash hit for the genius that is Gerry Anderson, *Stingray* featured more of Gerry's amazingly innovative filming techniques that drew you in and made you forget you were actually watching a puppet show. It was colourful, fast moving and beautifully written – and Atlanta Shore was the foxiest chick on the telly. See! She wasn't even real!

Stingray was set in the year 2065, where a Pacific Ocean dwelling super craft - crewed by futuristic heroes - raced around the seabed defeating monsters from inner space. The heroes were based at Marineville – a vast hi-tec complex founded on hydraulic platform that could descend into the Pacific Ocean in the event of attack.

571. 'Anything can happen –' complete the show's opening line.

572. Was the square jawed hero and pilot of *Stingray* called Troy or Kurt?

573. On which American actor was the puppet modelled - James Dean or James Garner?

574. George Sheridan was the navigator, but was his nickname Radar or Phones?

575. Stingray was an underwater ship for W.A.S.P. but what does it stand for? Was it Water-technic Advanced Systems Police or World Aquanaut Security Patrol?

576. Atlanta Shore was the commander's daughter, was her dad's name was Sam or Sandy?

577. The Aquaphibians were the wicked baddies, but who lead them - Neptune or Titan?

578. The Aquaphibians' secret spy was called Surface Agent X-2-Zero - true or false?

579. Was the beautiful mute girl who could breath underwater called Aqua Quay or Aqua Marina?

580. How many episodes were made - 12, 21, 39, or 45?

DID YOU KNOW?

Atlanta Shore was voiced by the amazing actress Lois Maxwell, most famous for playing the part of Miss Moneypenny in 14 of the James Bond films. She sadly departed in 2007.

Although never shown, the previous captain of Stingray was called Captain Grey who appeared in *Captain Scarlet*. And *Thunderbird 4* was written as being built by W.A.S.P.

BAGPUSS

'An old saggy, cloth cat. Baggy, and a bit loose at the seams'. Bagpuss was a quaint, stop frame animation programme set in a shop that didn't actually sell anything. Instead, a little girl would find lost things and place them in the window, next to her raggy old toy cat Bagpuss, so the owners could come and claim them. When she left, Bagpuss and the other toys would come to life and examine the objects. Another classic from Oliver Postgate and Peter Firmin's wonderful Smallfilms. Truly enchanting.

581. Name the little girl who owned Bagpuss - Edith, Emily or Eliza.

582. What colour were Bagpuss's stripes - red and blue, or pink and white?

583. Was the rag doll called Margaret or Madeline?

584. The wise wooden woodpecker book-end was Professor Yakkety - true or false?

585. In which year did *Bagpuss* first air 1965 - 1970 or 1974?

586. Gabriel the frog played which instrument - the piano, violin or banjo?

587. The mice were carved into the side of which instrument?

588. What did the mice chant when they fixed an object?

589. Derek Griffiths narrated the show - true or false?

590. How many episodes of *Bagpuss* were made -13, 26 or 49?

DID YOU KNOW?
The little girl who owned Bagpuss, seen at the beginning of every episode, was played by co-creator Peter Firmin's daughter. The original Bagpuss toy now resides in the Museum of Canterbury. The four lead mice were called Willie, Millie, Lizzie and Charlie, although it was never revealed on the show.

THE GOODIES

Should this even be in *The Classic Children's TV Quiz Book*? Was *The Goodies* a kids' show? Hard to say. In the special *The Goodies And The Beanstalk* Monty Python star John Cleese briefly plays a genie who mocks the show for being a '*kids' programme*'. What we do know is that kids, like adults, adored this surreal, slapstick, laugh-out-loud comedy starring Tim Brooke-Taylor, Bill Oddie and Graeme Garden. Whatever the show should be classed as, it was one of the finest British comedies of all time – so it's in!

591. Which Goodie was the mad inventor?
592. Was the Lancashire martial art from the episode *Kung Fu Capers* called Eeh-By-Gum-Foo, Ecky Thump or Barmpot Boxing?
593. Was the Goodies' three-seater tandem called Gertrude or Buttercup?
594. Where did they have the famous wild west style bun fight - the Doc Holliday Inn or the OK Tea Rooms?
595. Do you remember the catchy song they released about a funky primate?
596. Was the series originally going to be called *Superchaps 3* or *Helping Hands*?
597. In *Kitten Kong*, what London landmark did the giant kitten knock over - Big Ben or the Post Office Tower?
598. Counting specials, how many episodes of the Goodies were there - 24, 53 or 72?
599. Was Bill Oddie's 1989, short lived children's show, *The Bubblegum Brigade* or *Bill 'n' Birdy*?
600. Which of these is **NOT** a Christmas special, *The Goodies in Toyland*, *The Goodies and The Beanstalk*, *The Goodies Rule OK*?

DID YOU KNOW?
The Goodies ran from 1970 to 1980 on BBC1, then from 1981 to 1982 on ITV. A viewer in King's Lynn died whilst watching *The Goodies*. Alex Mitchell was laughing so much at the 1975 episode *Kung Fu Capers* he collapsed and expired. Anyone watching the glut of half thought out comedy shows on BBC3 might suffer the same fate – except the cause of death will either be boredom or embarrassment.

THE MAGIC ROUNDABOUT

'Boooiinng! Time for bed!' The Magic Roundabout began in 1964 in its original French incarnation *Le Manege Enchante* by Serge Danot. There were over 500 episodes made and shown in France. It was brought vividly to life for English speaking audiences by the late, great actor and voice artist Eric Thompson of *Play School* fame. Eric took the French episodes, minus the scripts and soundtracks, and made up stories based on what he saw. Eric, you were a bloody genius and we salute you!

601. Name the man who operated the roundabout - Mr Bolt or Mr Rusty?

602. Who was the bouncing jack-in-the box character?

603. The hippy rabbit was called Darren - true or false?

604. In which year did the English speaking version first air - 1960, 1965 or 1970?

605. Was the title of the 1974 film version *Dougal and the Blue Meany* or *Dougal and the Blue Cat*?

606. On which sardonic English comedian was Dougal the dog based - Kenneth Williams or Tony Hancock?

607. In the 2005 film version, which ex-Take That pop star voiced Dougal?

608. Was the cheery character Brian a slug or a snail?

609. Was the dippy, hat wearing cow called Gretchen or Ermintrude?

610. Which Young Ones actor narrated a further 52 episodes in 1992 - Rik Mayal or Nigel Planer?

DID YOU KNOW?
In the original French version Dougal was an English dog called Pollux who could only speak broken French.
Eric Thompson, the creator of the English version of *The Magic Roundabout* sadly passed away in 1982. He was father to the accomplished actresses Sophie Thompson and Emma Thompson.

I DON'T REMEMBER THAT! (5)

More argument fodder that didn't make it onto DVD or VHS, yet somehow made it onto You Tube.

Which show ...

611. Was a Canadian production about an ownerless German Shepherd dog who wandered from town to town helping people out? It was a film, a 1960s series, then brought back as a new series 1979 - 1983. ITV.

612. Had John Hurt as an other-worldly teller of tales recounting European fairy stories to his talking dog? Made by Jim Henson's company, the stories were told with a mixture of live action and puppets. ITV 1987.

613. Was a football based drama about the devoted junior fans of Dunmore United and their relationship with the often demoralised manager Mac Murphy? The catchy theme was sung by the late Gary Holton of *Auf Wiedersehen Pet* fame. ITV 1982 – 1985.

614. Was based on a Terry Pratchett novel about Johnny Maxwell who fights to save a local cemetery from being bulldozed so his new friends, the dead, won't become homeless? The ever wonderful Brian Blessed starred. ITV 1995.

615. Revolved around a cheeky robot who lived with the very ordinary Wilberforce family as a domestic help? Created by their son, the robot was more a hindrance than a help, but they loved him, especially Gran, played by the late comedy legend Irene Handl (1901–1987). ITV 1980.

616. Featured a mixture of animal and human model characters who inhabited a magical, walled garden? The central character in this, classic stop-motion animation, show was a friendly, mute lion. BBC 1968.

617. Was a long running anthology series which had contributions from many different regional ITV franchise holders such as Tyne-Tees, Scottish and Granada? The one-off stories were usually of a science fiction or supernatural flavour. ITV 1983 - 1989.

618. Centred around a home for retired or unwanted horses with Dora, Steve, Ron and Slugger looking after them? It was based on a novel by Monica Dickens, great granddaughter of Charley, and had a brilliant theme tune called *The Lightning Tree*. ITV 1972 – 1973.

619. Was a cartoon about a young elephant who bit his mother's fountain pen whilst having a bath and, as a result, was dyed blue? This made it hard for him to fit into the world of humans – so nothing to do with him being a talking elephant then? ITV 1976.

620. Was co-devised by evil sorcerer Paul Daniels and saw a large, cheery, alien wizard's hat, and his huge rabbit friend Wooly, learning about life on Earth in Puzzleopolis? Viewers got to solve logic problems with the characters. BBC 1986 – 1988.

BATMAN – THE TV SERIES

Atomic batteries to power, turbines to speed! The Batmobile - with the Caped Crusader and the Boy Wonder safely buckled in - minced into life in 1968 and gave us 120 psychedelic, heart thumping, lens twisting, brightly coloured adventures. POW! It was like nothing we'd seen before and we loved it! *BAM!* Catwoman, The Riddler, The Joker and The Penguin became the criminal world's leading exponents of highly camp, and deeply flawed, dastardly plans. *BOP!*

621. **Who played Batman so deliciously in this series - Leonard Nimoy or Adam West?**

622. **Was Bruce Wayne's faithful English butler called Arnold or Alfred?**

623. **In the show, what was Robin's real name - Don Gregson or Dick Grayson?**

624. **Which actor played the part of Robin - Butch Patrick or Burt Ward?**

625. **Can you remember the Police Commissioner's surname - was it Gordon, London or Beefeater?**

626. **What family relation was Batgirl to the Commissioner?**

627. **Which amazing actor played the original Riddler in the show - Frank Gorshin or Roddy McDowall?**

628. **Was the Irish Police Chief called O'Rafferty or O'Hara?**

629. **Burgess Meredith played The Joker - true or false?**

630. **Which actress *didn't* play Catwoman - Joan Collins, Julie Newmar or Eartha Kitt?**

DID YOU KNOW?
Alan Napier (1903–1988) played Bruce Wayne's butler throughout the series. Born in Birmingham, Alan was the cousin of British Prime Minister Neville Chamberlain and the great, great grandson of Charles Dickens. *Holy British Aristocracy, Batman!* And, in the 1989 film Batman, the Joker's real name was given as Jack Napier, a salute to Alan Napier.

TELETUBBIES

(1997–2001) Devised by Anne Wood and Andrew Davenport, Teletubbies was a, some might say surreal, pre-school programme about four toddler type creatures who have TV screens in their tummies and different shaped antennae on their heads. The show used baby talk, songs, rhymes, bright colours and repetition to appeal to children from nought upwards. It was a smash hit world wide so let's all give each other a *big hug*, answer the questions *again* and *again*, and then run away!

631. How do the Teletubbies greet one another?

632. What colour was Po?

633. Can you remember what the helpful vacuum cleaner was called - The Noo-Noo or The Dyson-Wyson?

634. The scooter belonged to which Teletubbie?

635. Name the Teletubbie who had a huge, orange ball.

636. What furry creatures shared Teletubbyland with the gang - rabbits, squirrels or guinea pigs?

637. What colour was Laa-Laa?

638. Name the company that produced the show - Jim Henson Productions, Ragdoll or Cosgrove Hall?

639. What colour was Dipsy?

640. How many episodes were made before it was *time for Tubby bye bye* - 165, 265 or 365?

DID YOU KNOW?
In America, *Teletubbies* was blasted by The Reverend Jerry Falwell who accused Tinky Winky of being gay. The reasons being Tinky Winky was a boy but had a handbag, and his purple triangular antennae is similar to the symbol of the Gay Pride movement. Was the Reverend being overly suspicious about the show? Well, Dipsy's huge, camp, black and white hat did look like something Boy George would wear – *uh-oh!*

ROD HULL AND EMU

Rod Hull (1935 – 1999) was a one-man children's television institution and gave us many years of anarchic, spontaneous fun as his darker alter-ego, his vicious pet bird Emu, attacked, destroyed and caused general pandemonium everywhere it went. When Rod and Emu appeared on telly it was an unmissable event – you couldn't guess what was going to happen - but when you saw Emu's beak curl up you just knew the emu poo was about to hit the fan.

641. Did Rod use his left or right arm to animate Emu?

642. Did Emu have his own catchphrase?

643. Name Rod's 1975 BBC show, it's initials were E.B.C.

644. What colour was the Windmill where Rod's 1986 show came from?

645. In the Windmill shows, which witch was always trying to steal Emu -Witchiepoo, Fenella Fellorick, or Grotbags?

646. What colour was she - blue, orange or green?

647. Recite the chant we all cried when someone came to call.

648. Which English chat show host did Emu famously attack in 1976?

649. On Channel 4's *The Word*, which American rapper did Emu attack - Ice T or Snoop Dog?

650. How old was Rod Hull when he died - 42, 57, 63 or 70?

DID YOU KNOW?
Many thought the legendary Rod Hull was Australian, but he was English. He moved to Australia in the 1960s after training to be an electrician. Rod Hull sadly died in March 1996, after falling from his roof which he had climbed up to in order to adjust his television aerial. Bloody Emu, always took a joke too far.

WHOSE VOICE *IS* THAT? (2)

Another selection of stinkers from the files subtitled 'Oooh I bloody well know that voice, it's him off that show about the whatnot set in the thingy place.'

651.	*Bleep and Booster* (1963)	**Jon Pertwee**
652.	*Henry's Cat* (1983)	**Andrew Sachs**
653.	*Huxley Pig* (1989)	**Bernard Cribbins**
654.	*William's Wish Wellingtons* (1992)	**Lionel Jeffries**
655.	*Towser* (1982)	**Bob Godfrey**
656.	*Grizzly Tales for Gruesome Kids* (2000)	**Peter Ustinov**
657.	*The Little Green Man* (1989)	**Nigel Planer**
658.	*Simon in The Land of Chalk Drawings* (1974)	**Peter Hawkins**
659.	*Doctor Snuggles* (1980)	**Roy Kinnear**
660.	*Fred Basset* (1976)	**Martin Jarvis**

DID YOU KNOW?
Actor John Challis, Boycie from *Only Fools and Horses* and *Green Green Grass*, provided voices for Doctor Snuggles (1980), which, incidentally boasted Douglas Adams as one of its writers. Having a big name doing voices for an animation show is no guarantee of success. For example, do you remember Terry Wogan narrating a 1988 show called *Stoppit and Tidyup*? Or Dudley Moore voicing *Oscar's Orchestra* in 1994. No? Neither do we.

DANGERMOUSE

Dangermouse – powerhouse! You just knew the cartoon world was a safer place thanks to the dashing secret agent Dangermouse and his faithful sidekick hamster Penfold. Kicking off in 1981, *Dangermouse* was another high flying success for the wonderful Cosgrove Hall and for many people is THE greatest kids' show ever produced. It was the first British cartoon to break the States too.

661. Was Dangermouse's secret London hideout disguised as a phone box or a post box?

662. On which famous London street was the hideout - Oxford Road or Baker Street?

663. Name the crème-de-la-crème comedy actor who voiced Dangermouse.

664. When June let him, who voiced Penfold - John Inman, Terry Scott or Windsor Davies?

665. Who was the dastardly green villain of the piece - Baron Silas Greenback or Lord Warty Toadback?

666. Was the villain's white, furry pet caterpillar called Caesar, Caligula or Nero?

667. Was the villain's main henchman - a crow - called Slingback or Stiletto?

668. Dangermouse had a crusty, forgetful old boss - was he Colonel X, Q or K?

669. The M type character who designed all Dangermouse's gadgets was Professor Heinrich Von Squawkencluck - true or false?

670. How many episodes were made - 16, 50, 89 or 209?

DID YOU KNOW?
The brilliantly catchy *Dangermouse* theme song was composed by legendary comedian Mike Harding. It was sung by Myfanwy Talog (1945 – 1995) who was the long term partner of David Jason.
Another Cosgrove Hall hit cartoon character, Count Duckula, started out in *Dangermouse* as a recurring villain. His first appearance was in *The Four Tasks of Dangermouse*.
The mono-sighted special agent wore his eye patch over his left eye although he freely admitted there was no need for it, both eyes worked perfectly.
Penfold's first name was Ernest.

THE TOMORROW PEOPLE

Human evolution is slowly moving forward and a new breed of telepathic, super intelligent humans are emerging, *The Tomorrow People*.
Whatever anyone tells you, there has *NEVER* been scarier titles to a TV show than the original Tomorrow People. The spooky imagery coming towards you (*the hand! good God, remember the opening hand!*) and amazingly atmospheric music sent shivers down the spine of many a young person in the 1970s. Created by Roger Price, *The Tomorrow People* really is in the top 10 for the ultimate sci-fi experience. (*Jesus, remember that bloody hand!*)

671. What was the term used for an emerging Tomorrow Person, Coming Through or Breaking Out?

672. Was their secret base called The Lab or The Lair?

673. Their base was situated in an old abandoned London what - a WW2 Bunker or Underground Station?

674. How did they describe their method of teleportation - Beaming, Flitting or Jaunting?

675. Was the biological super computer who assisted the team TOMTIT or TIM?

676. Who was the dark haired, older, leader of the Tomorrow People - Mark, Luke or John?

677. And which actor played him - Karl Howman or Nicholas Young?

678. Was the first story entitled *The Slaves Of Jedikiah* or *A New Kind of Man*?

679. What species of human beings were the Tomorrow People - ManMark2 or Homo-Superior?

680. Have quadruple points if you know the David Bowie song this term also appears in - *Kooks* or *Oh! You Pretty Things*?

DID YOU KNOW?
In the show, we normal human beings were referred to as Saps, short for homosapien – how patronising is that?!
So far there have been three incarnations of the show. The original show 1973 – 1979, a re-imagined TV series 1992 -1995, and an audio version of the original series made by Big Finish in 2001.

CHUCKLE BROTHERS

The Chuckle Brothers, or just the 'Chucks' because we love them so much, have been an enduring act in children's telly for many years and in the 21st century they're like a breath of old air in the face of P.C., moral laden, sanitised kids' programming – you hearing this America? Hearty slapstick, puns, and dim-witted antics are what these two veterans dish out and young and old sit glued to their shows in their millions. They really should be knighted for their services to children's TV, and that's NOT a joke. But, can you imagine the right royal debacle they'd cause! Someone would get stabbed with the knighting sword, with hilarious consequences! *Oh dear oh dear!*

681. What are the Christian names of the Chuckle Brothers - Ron and George, Ken and Wally or Paul and Barry?
682. Are they from Middlesbrough, Rotherham, Aberdeen or London?
683. On which 1974 talent show did they first appear - *Opportunity Knocks* or *New Faces*?
684. For their 1985 show they dressed as dogs, was the series called *The Chucklehounds, The Chuckpuppies* or *The Chuckling Bow Wows*?
685. How many episodes did they do as dogs - 3, 13, 33 or 133?
686. In what year did Chucklevision start -1987, 1988 or 1989?
687. You must know their catchphrase?
688. Name their CBBC gameshow set on a desert Island.
689. What years did the gameshow run from 1986-88 or 1996-98?
690. Have double points if you know the Chucks' real surname - Houston, Elliot, Garner or Paragon?

DID YOU KNOW?
Comedian and actor Jimmy Patton appears regularly in *Chucklevision*, usually as the foil for the brothers, i.e. their employer or an authority figure who falls foul of the bungling twosome. His catchphrase in the show is '*And remember, no slacking*'. Jimmy is actually Paul and Barry's older brother. Another older brother, Brian Patton occasionally appears too.
An unsung hero of the Chucks, and CBBC in general, is their long time director and producer Martin Hughes who retired from the TV industry in 2004.

I DON'T REMEMBER THAT! (6)

Some more shows to rattle your brains trying to remember before giving up, cheating and saying 'Ooooh, I bloody well knew that!'

Which show ...

691.   Was a Saturday morning magazine show fronted by bubbly Cheryl from Bucks Fizz? It had an entertaining mix of cookery, pop music and celebrities. Often shown before *Live and Kicking*. BBC, 1988 – 1993.

692.   Was an American cartoon about a grumpy sailor who gained amazing strength from eating a certain kind of vegetable? Rumour has it he enjoyed eating olives too. **ALL CHANNELS 1933 onward.**

693.   Was created by the legendary John Cunliffe and Ivor Wood and centred around a friendly postal service operative called Mr Clifton and his pet cat? BBC 1981 onward.

694.   ' - - *The Series*', was one of many vehicles for this sarky glove puppet? He was quick witted, big headed and a joy to watch for all ages and was brought into being to save the ailing TV-AM. This show BBC 1986.

695.   Focused on a society of blue, miniature, white hat wearing people living in a beautiful woodland village made up of mushroomed shaped houses? BBC 1981 (although there are films and series dating back to the 1950s).

696. Was about a group of Victorian street urchins and snipes who helped out Sherlock Holme? A young Adam (*EastEnders*) Woodyatt played Shiner. BBC 1983.

697. Was a gentle, black and white show about three glove puppet creatures - a hedgehog, a mouse and a rabbit? Shown as part of the legendary umbrella *Watch With Mother*. BBC 1953 – 1965.

698. Starred Clive 'don't panic' Dunn as an interfering, but loveable old caretaker of a community hall? A sitcom written by Bob *'Rentaghost'* Block. BBC 1979 – 1984.

699. Is *the* longest running American TV series combining live action, puppets and animation to make an educational pre-school show? It's never really caught on in Britain probably because of its gushy sentimentality. Shown on ITV and Channel 4. Broadcast in USA 1969 – present.

700. Had a hideous wooden puppet that spoke in semi-English, semi-nonsense and lived inside your telly? He gobbed on the screen at the start of each show and wrote his name in the condensation. Celebrities visited his garden. Channel 4 1985 – 1990.

SATURDAY MORNING TV (1)

Remember when Saturday morning telly was appointment TV? You would sit there with the remote flitting from BBC to ITV trying to watch two brilliant shows at once. There were no video recorders or Sky Plus or Virgin Players back then, oh no. And now we have every opportunity to view 21st century Saturday morning shows anytime we wish.....well, what's the point? Match the classic Saturday morning telly shows with the year they first *started*.

701.	*Going Live*	1982
702.	*Swap Shop*	1993
703.	*No. 73*	1998
704.	*Ministry of Mayhem*	1990
705.	*Tiswas*	1986
706.	*Get Fresh*	1976
707.	*Live And Kicking*	1987
708.	*Dick And Dom in Da Bunglaow*	1974
709.	*SMTV Live*	2003
710.	*The 8.15 from Manchester*	2004

DID YOU KNOW?
In the 1986 show *Get Fresh*, snotty Gilbert The Alien was voiced by comedian Phil Cornwell.
In 1982 there was a rude, late night version of *Tiswas* called O.T.T.
Before he went bonkers, David Icke was in the sports department of *Saturday Superstore*. Icke sacrificed his credibility and his journalistic career for his new age beliefs, and fair play to him for his convictions. Mind you, he does think The Queen, George Bush and Boxcar Willie are reptilian, shape shifting aliens. The silly sod.

SATURDAY MORNING TV (2)

Remember when our favourite Saturday morning shows took the summer off and we got something that wasn't quite as good, seemingly deliberately so. Imagine offering the presenters the jobs for these summer stand ins – 'It doesn't matter if you're a bit rubbish, everyone's on holiday anyway.' Still, we council house kids who couldn't afford Spanish summer holidays loved them. Anyway, match the ORIGINAL presenters with these classic Saturday morning shows?

711.	*Motormouth*	**Zoe Ball, Grant Scott**
712.	*No. 73*	**Emma Forbes,**
		Andi Peters
713.	*Ministry of Mayhem*	**Neil Buchanan**
714.	*Going Live*	**Jenny Powell,**
		Nobby the Sheep
715.	*Saturday Superstore*	**Ant, Dec and Cat**
716.	*Parallel 9*	**Phillip Schofield,**
		Sarah Greene
717.	*Live And Kicking*	**Stephen Mulhern,**
		Holly Willoughby
718.	*SMTV Live*	**Mike Reid**
719.	*Gimme 5*	**Sandi Toksvig**
720.	*Fully Booked*	**Mercator The Alien**

DID YOU KNOW?
The theme for the *8.15 From Manchester* (BBC1 1990) was by Inspiral Carpets, a reworking of their song *Find Out Why*.
Another show, *On The Waterfront* (BBC 1987) boasted an overdubbed version of *The Flashing Blade* scripted by Doctor Who re-creator Russell T. Davies. Other Saturday morning shows you might recall: *Saturday Starship, Get Set for Summer, Scratchy and Co, Our Show, The Saturday Picture Show, Ghost Train, It's Wicked* and *Teleganticmegavision*.

THUNDERBIRDS

5 – 4 – 3 – 2 – 1! Thunderbirds are go! Gerry Anderson's groundbreaking puppet show blasted off in 1965 and had viewers on the edge of their seats with its dazzling special effects and astoundingly realistic models. The heroic rescue pilots saved the world from disasters, accidents and sabotage and were quite literally F.A.B! (F.A.B. stood for Funderbirds Are Brill – well, that's what I was told.)

721. What organisation did the show revolve around?

722. Was the millionaire, ex-astronaut, father of the pilots called Wayne or Jeff Tracy?

723. On which island did the family of heroes reside on?

724. What type of craft was Thunderbird 4 - a submarine or rocket plane?

725. Which of these was not a character - Alan, Virgil, Sam, Gordon.

726. What type of craft was Thunderbird 5 - a space station or heavy duty lifting jet?

727. Name the scientific engineer and advisor - Poindexter or Brains?

728. Who was the posh female London agent?

729. Can you remember her chauffeur's name?

730. FAB1 was the registration of their pink, modified car, but what make was it?

DID YOU KNOW?
Inspiration for *Thunderbirds* came from Thunderbird Field, an American air base where Anderson's brother was stationed during WW2.
Lady Penelope's car may have been FAB1, but FAB2 was her yacht and FAB3 was her prize winning racehorse.
Thunderbird 6 was an old bi-plane. *Thunderbirds* the TV series is considered a classic, but the Thunderbirds films seem to be beyond rescue of any kind. The first movie, *Thunderbirds Are Go*, flopped in 1966, and the 2004 live action version was panned by critics.

CHILDREN OF THE STONES

Mention *Children of the Stones* to anyone who watched TV in the 1970s and you're guaranteed a reaction of well remembered fear. A father and son temporarily move to a mysterious English village and encounter danger from the mists of time in the shape of megalithic stone circles, time dilation and rampaging druids.

Even in the 21st century, the show still holds its own in terms of sinister ambience and terror - in much the same way *Sapphire and Steel* does -mainly because it didn't over use limited special effects of the day and concentrated on superb dialogue, enthralling storytelling and ingenious production and direction. Also, the terrifying musical score – by Sidney Sager (1917 – 2002) put the willies up us all!

731. What was Mr Brake's profession - astrophysicist or professor of occult studies?

732. Name the village Mr Brake and his son moved to - Milbury or Thornaby?

733. What was the son's first name - Matthew or Marcus?

734. At the beginning, how many stones surrounded the village - 53 or 1,003?

735. In what year did this series first run - 1977 or 1987?

736. What did the eerie villagers say instead of hello and goodbye - *Happy day* or *Golden day*?

737. What was the evil Mr Hendrick's first name - Gabriel, Ariel or Rafael?

738. Which superb actor played the poacher Dai - Freddie Jones or Peter Sallis?

739. How many episodes were there in this one-off series - five, seven or nine?

740. Did *Children of the Stones* first air on ITV or the BBC?

DID YOU KNOW?
Gareth Thomas went on to play the eponymous Blake in the wonderful Terry Nation sci-fi show *Blake's 7*. Gareth had a non speaking part right at the very beginning of another spooky classic, the Nigel Neale film version of *Quatermass and The Pit* (1967). *Children of the Stones* is available on DVD, you really have to get a copy.

FROM BIG SCREEN TO SMALL SCREEN

Sometimes the worlds of telly and cinema converge and we get smaller budgeted versions of our favourite big screen classics with look-a-like actors and shark jumping plotlines. And in American cases usually just an animated attempt at recapturing the movie magic. Mind you, they do sometimes get it right, *Star Trek: The Animated Series* (1973) was brilliant. And the 1975 cartoon *Return to the Planet of the Apes* was actually not half bad. But, do you remember the 1974 *Planet of the Apes* TV series based on the 1968 Charlton Heston sci-fi film classic? The live action telly version meandered along for 14 formulaic episodes before someone put an end to its monkey business.

These films were eventually made into kids' TV shows - true or false?

741.	*Ace Ventura Pet Detective*	True / False
742.	*Monsters Inc*	True / False
743.	*Honey I Shrunk the Kids*	True / False
744.	*Ghostbusters*	True / False
745.	*Jumanji*	True / False
746.	*Agent Cody Banks*	True / False
747.	*The Railway Children*	True / False
748.	*The Mask*	True / False
749.	*Chitty Chitty Bang Bang*	True / False
750.	*Harry and the Hendersons*	True / False

DID YOU KNOW?
Chitty Chitty Bang Bang was written by Ian Fleming, who also created James Bond.
Ray Parker Jnr, who wrote the catchy *Ghostbusters* theme, was sued by Huey Lewis for stealing the tune from him. Who y'gonna call, Ray, y'lawyer? Other films turned into telly shows have been: *Back To The Future*, *Clueless*, *Aladdin*, *Star Wars*, *Godzilla*, *Men In Black* and *Indiana Jones*.

HONG KONG PHOOEY

Number one superguy *Hong Kong Phooey* karate kicked his way onto our screens in 1974 in the heyday of martial arts fever brought about by Bruce Lee and the Carl Douglas hit *Kung Fu Fighting*. Another Hanna-Barbera classic, *Hong Kong Phooey* centred around a bungling crime fighting dog whose long suffering sidekick cat always saved the day, but was never recognised, or even thanked for it.

751.   What was Hong Kong Phooey's alias - Penrod Pooch or Percy Puppy?

752.   At the Police Station, he was the mild mannered jailer - true or false?

753.   What did he leap into in order to change into Hong Kong Phooey - a trash can or a filing cabinet?

754.   Who was the officer in charge of the Police Station - Sergeant Flint or Sergeant Stones?

755.   Name H.K.P 's faithful sidekick cat - Stripe, Star or Spot?

756.   The telephone operator had a crush on H.K.P. - was she Carol or Rosemary?

757.   What was his amazing, transforming car called - The Phooeymobile or The Karate Chop Suey Wagon?

758.   How would H.K.P. transform the style of the vehicle - with a magic incantation or by banging on a gong?

759.   **NOT** a H.K.P. villain: Batty Bank Mob, Candy Bandit, Cat Napper or Tin Nose?

760.   If he got stuck, which training manual did he pull out of his sleeve and check - *The Bruce Lee Book of Masterful Moves* or *The Hong Kong Book of Kung-Fu?*

DID YOU KNOW?
Hong Kong Phooey was voiced by legendary American actor and singer Scatman Crothers (1910 – 1986) who had a distinguished career in film and TV, starring in many shows such as *Bewitched*, *Kolchak: The Night Stalker* and *Magnum P.I.* He also voiced Autobot Jazz in the 1984 cartoon series of *Transformers*. Scatman we salute you!
The legendary animator, character designer and producer Iwao Takamoto (1925 –2007) – who designed *Scooby Doo* - produced H.K.P. Iwao learned his artistic skills in an American internment camp during WW2 when his family were sent there after the bombing of Pearl Harbour. We salute you too, Iwao!

THE WOMBLES

In the 1970s, the Wombles were way ahead of their time, hammering home the green message of recycling. Whatever we humans threw away the Wombles would collect and reuse. Their motto was *make good use of bad rubbish*. A very worthy way of life, but one can't help thinking, they must have stank. Made by FilmFair with stop animation, *The Wombles* was an instant hit and kids all over the country began to take care of their environment. For a bit. And thanks to pop impresario Mike Batt the furry, big-nosed, eco-pioneers even released a couple of rather good records too.

761. On which London common did the Wombles live?

762. Was the crusty, but kind, leader of the Wombles Great Uncle Hungary or Bulgaria?

763. Name the French female Womble chef - Madame Cholet or Oohlala?

764. Which top comedy actor voiced the original series, Kenneth Williams, Frankie Howerd or Bernard Cribbens?

765. Was the caretaker and inventor of the Wombles clan - Tobermory or Balamory?

766. The writer who created *The Wombles* - was it Helen Cresswell or Elisabeth Beresford?

767. Who was the laziest Womble - Orlando, Orinoco or Oregano?

768. Complete the phrase *Underground overground Wombling free --*

769. The bespectacled brainy young Womble was called Gumboot - true or false?

770. In what year did the series first air - 1967, 1973 or 1979?

DOCTOR WHO – THE NEW SERIES

Christopher Eccelstone hit the ground running as the good Doctor returned to our screens in 2005. Re-creator Russell T. Davies delivered to the old fans an old and deeply missed friend, and to the legions of new Who fans he gave a level of science fiction drama that would change their lives forever. The skilful quill wielder Steven Moffat took over the production helm in late 2008 so you don't need a time machine to know the future of Doctor is a bright and 'Rosey' one.

771.   What number Doctor did Ecclestone play?

772.   Which war wiped out the Doctor's people, the Time Lords - was it The Dalek Massacres or The Time War?

773.   In the new series, who was the Doctor's first companion Martha or Rose?

774.   Name Catherine Tate's character - was it Diane Nubile or Donna Noble?

775.   Which 1970s' companion came back in the episode School Reunion - Jo Grant or Sarah Jane Smith?

776.   Which character had immortality thrust upon him - Mickey Smith or Captain Jack?

777.   Which two actors played the Master in series three?

778.   Name Kylie Minogue's character in the 2007 Christmas Special - Astrid Peth or Asteroid Bondi?

779.   Give yourself a double points if you can give David Tennant's real name.

780.   Give yourself a quadruple points if you can name the Slitheen home planet.

H.R. PUFNSTUF

Lured to a magical island where most things such as animals, trees, houses, candles - you name it - were alive, a little boy is stranded and trying not to fall foul of an evil witch and her cohorts. Taken under the wing of the big friendly Mayor of the island, they had bright, fast paced, singing, dancing, psychedelic adventures each week as they tried to get the kid home. A young Jack Wilde (1952 – 2006) skilfully played the English boy, and you might also remember him from the role of the Artful Dodger in the 1968 smash hit musical Oliver! We salute you Jack!

781. Can you remember the lost little boy's name - Timmy or Jimmy?

782. How did he get to the island - by magic carpet, helicopter or boat?

783. Was Pufnstuff a huge talking cake, dragon, or mushroom?

784. Name the island where almost everything was alive - Sentient Peninsula or Living Island?

785. Who was the wicked witch who taunted the good guys each week - Witchiepoo or The White Witch Jadis?

786. What was the witch's jet powered broom vehicle called - The Rush Brush or The Vroom Broom?

787. In what year did *H.R. Pufnstuf* first air -1959, 1969 or 1979?

788. The lost young boy had a talking flute called Teddy, Freddie or Neddy?

789. Which legendary cowboy film star did the west wind sound like - Robert Mitchum or John Wayne?

790. How many episodes, not counting the film, were made - 17, 67 or 107?

DID YOU KNOW?
Like many classic TV shows, a myth has built up around H.R. Pufnstuff. In this case (like Mr Benn and The Magic Roundabout) it's thought the entire show was about taking drugs, a claim its creators Sid and Marty Krofft neither confirm nor deny. Mind you the name hasn't helped the show's image, Pufnstuff sounds exactly like 'puffing stuff' and H.R. is thought to mean 'Hand Rolled.' Legend has it H.R. is actually Royal Highness backwards.

CATWEAZLE

Another wonderful and enthralling slice of TV history from the pen of Richard 'The Ghosts of Motley Hall' Carpenter. Catweazle was a half mad and utterly useless magician who falls through time as he is chased by soldiers. He leaps from a castle's battlements into a moat and emerges in the 20th century, scared, befuddled, but glad to be alive. There were two series and in each one the shabby, shameless shaman is befriended by a long suffering 20th century boy. Played to blissful perfection by the legendary Geoffrey Bayldon, Catweazle is still a delight to watch. Get it on DVD, you will NOT be disappointed! Mister Bayldon and Mr Carpenter, we salute you!

791. From which century did Catweazle escape to the 20th century - the 5th, 8th or 11th?

792. Who was Catweazle running from - Romans, Vikings or Normans?

793. In series one, was the young boy's nickname Parsnip, Sprout or Carrot?

794. In series two, was the young boy's nickname Owlface, Divlegs or Ratsteeth?

795. Infuriated at his own magic failures, was Catweazle's catchphrase *Nothing works* or *Failure upon failure*?

796. In what year did series one air - 1969, 1970, 1971 or 1972?

797. How many episodes of *Catweazle* were there altogether - 12, 19, 26 or 30?

798. Touchwood was Catweazle's scaly familiar, what type of creature was it?

799. What did Catweazle call the telephone - *the telling-bone* or *the arc of voices*?

800. What did he name the abandoned water tower where he lived - Fort Mage or Castle Saburac?

DID YOU KNOW?
Geoffrey Bayldon has had many dalliances with TV's *Doctor Who*. He turned down the part of the first Doctor Who, but did appear in a few episodes later on. He went on to play the temporal ticket inspector in the Big Finish audio plays *Doctor Who Unbound*. Aha! So is it a coincidence then that his familiar in *Catweazle* was called Touchwood, one letter away from Torchwood – which is an anagram of Doctor Who! Hey? Well? Hmm? Yes, it is a coincidence. Actually.

TOP CAT

Top Cat, the indisputable leader of the gang! And he was! Smooth talking, fast acting, and always landing on his feet. Top Cat seemed to be the cat with more than nine lives as he evaded the law, kept his gang fed, and always had time for the underdog. Even today, the catchy, sing-a-long, big band theme tune raises a smile and brings back wonderful memories of this classic cartoon.

801. Top Cat wore a bowler hat - true or false?

802. Who was the Police officer whose beat took him through the alley - Sneeble or Dibble?

803. In which American city did the cats live - San Francisco or New York?

804. In the opening titles, what does T.C. have on a string?

805. Also in the titles, what does T.C. steal from the workman in the hole?

806. Which cat was the considered the dimmest - Spook or Brain?

807. Who made the show - Disney, Hanna-Barbera or Warner Brothers?

808. How many episodes were made - 20, 30, 40 or 50?

809. NOT a member of the gang - Fancy-Fancy, Mange, Choo Choo?

810. What was the show renamed so it could air in Britain?

DID YOU KNOW?
The premise for the show was taken from *The Phil Silvers Show* (1955), indeed the character of Top Cat is very similar to Sgt Bilko and voice over artist Arnold Stang based Top Cat's voice on Silvers.
Benny The Ball was actually voiced by Maurice Gosfield who played Private Duane Doberman in *The Phil Silvers Show*, a character not a million miles away from Benny. *Top Cat* had to be re-titled in Britain so as not to be seen as an endorsement of the cat food Top-Cat. Now that brand is no longer made, repeats of the show have deferred to its original name.

FROM PAGE TO SMALL SCREEN

A TV or film adaptation of a book is a great way to encourage kids to read more. Look how many children rushed out to buy *Harry Potter & The Need For An Editor*, before deciding the bloody thing was far too long to tackle. It seems every popular book gets made into something nowadays – heck this very quiz book would make a great disaster movie. Yes, books and TV are inexorably linked, so let's just hope the classics aren't updated too much for our modern computer age. TV serials like *Charlotte's Web Page, The Jpeg Of Dorian Gray, Cyber With Rosie, Of Mice Mats and Men*, and *The Canterbury Emails* might not have the same impact as the original books they were based on.

These children's books were eventually made into TV shows - true or false?

811.	*Stig Of The Dump*	True / False
812.	*Mary Poppins*	True / False
813.	*Chocky*	True / False
814.	*Harry Potter*	True / False
815.	*Black Beauty*	True / False
816.	*The Lion, The Witch and The Wardrobe*	True / False
817.	*His Dark Materials*	True / False
818.	*Charlie and The Chocolate Factory*	True / False
819.	*Danny Champion of the World*	True / False
820.	*The Machine Gunners*	True / False

DID YOU KNOW?
In the original version of Roald Dahl's book *Charlie and The Chocolate Factory* the Oompa-loompas were black skinned pygmies from Africa who worked for cacao (cocoa) beans. Because this was deemed racist, Dahl changed the text in 1973 to make them white skinned and from Loompaland.

THE SINGING RINGING TREE

Haunting, magical, mind blowing and downright scary, *The Singing Ringing Tree* is something that evokes a gamut of emotions from anyone who has seen it. Made in post war East Germany, this film was transmitted in Britain broken up into a serial with an English narrator explaining what was going on – or at least having a go! – rather than being dubbed. It's incredibly surreal and doesn't have much dialogue anyway. It is, however, visually stunning and must have broken the bank when it came to the budget for sets, costumes and make up. It tells the story of a lovelorn Prince trying to win the heart of a snotty cow of a Princess by bringing her the fabled Singing Ringing Tree. They both fall foul of an evil Dwarf – who looks like a miniaturised youthful Peter Cook – and are trapped in his realm. It's well worth another look and is available on DVD.

821.   What will the Tree do if the Princess truly loves the Prince?

822.   What kind of beast was the handsome Prince turned into - a lion or a bear?

823.   Does the Dwarf turn the Prince's horse into vines, glass or stone?

824.   Is the lake dwelling, oversized creature a fish, a toad or a snake?

825.   How did the Dwarf try to kill this aquatic creature - with a harpoon, or by freezing the lake?

826.   What does the Dwarf steal away from the Princess - her youth or her beauty?

827.   Was the entrance to the Dwarf's world a musical bridge or a disappearing stone?

828.   Making a shelter, does the Bear dig out a cave or build a wooden hut?

829.   Does the Dwarf surround the Singing Ringing Tree with goblins, fire or ice to protect it?

830.   What year was this classic presentation made - 1948, 1959, 1961 or 1968?

DID YOU KNOW?
When it was made, *The Singing Ringing Tree* narrowly escaped being heavily censored by the (then) Communist government as it was found to glorify the bourgeois idea of monarchy. Other such traditional fairy stories were indeed changed to show the lower classes - like shoemakers and woodcutters - to be the real heroes, never the aristocracy. The daft Eastern Blockheads that they were.

BUTTON MOON

This charming little show must have had THE smallest budget of any telly programme ever. The set and characters looked like they were cobbled together from whatever the creators found lying around their kitchens – and this was before recycling became politically correct. That said, that good old *Button Moon*, with its fantastically creative characters, remains one of the most endearing and magical places we ever visited through our portals in the corner.

831. In what sky did Button Moon shine - Blanket Sky, Duvet Sky, or Sheet Sky?

832. Which adventurer blasted off for Button Moon every week - Mr Ladle or Mr Spoon?

833. What was his daughter called - Tina, Tallulah, or Tabitha?

834. She had a friend - was he called Edgar, Elidor, or Eggbert?

835. Can you remember what planet they came from - Junk Planet, Trash-Teroid, or Rubbish World?

836. Their rocket was made from what type of food tin - a hot dog tin, a custard tin, or a baked bean tin?

837. To see stories, what did they look through - a collideascope or a telescope?

838. Which company made it -Tyne Tees, Anglia, Thames Television or ATV?

839. Were there more, or less than, 100 episodes made?

840. Was the narrator Robin Parkinson or Michael Parkinson?

DID YOU KNOW?
The theme tune was sung and composed by the 5th Doctor Who Peter Davison, and his then wife Sandra Dickinson. Peter and Sandra also appeared together in *The Hitchhikers Guide to the Galaxy* (1981) in the *Restaurant at the End of the Universe* scene. She played Trillian, he played a talkative cow who convinced diners to eat him.

SUPERGRAN

Stand back Superman, Iceman, Spiderman, Batman and Robin too! Supergran was a Tyne Tees offering featuring a gentle old Scottish granny who is accidentally given superhero-like powers when one of Inventor Black's amazing devices is misused. From then on crime doesn't stand a chance when the super fast, super strong wrinkly has cashed her pension and is ready for action.

841. What was Supergran's real name - Nana McDither or Granny Smith?

842. She got her powers after being accidentally hit by a magic ray - true or false?

843. Was her young grandson called Bertram, Norbert, or Willard?

844. Name the fictional town it was set in - Flumock-on-the-Cree or Chisleton?

845. How many episodes were made - 6, 27, 56 or 101?

846. Who was the recurring Scottish baddy played by Iain C Cuthbertson - was it Sawney Bean, The Tartan Terror, or The Scunner Campbell?

847. Inventor Black had a granddaughter called Edison - true or false?

848. Which Scottish comedian wrote and sang the catchy theme tune?

849. Which actress played Supergran - Annette Crosbie or Gudrun Ure?

850. In which year did the show first air - 1970, 1979 or 1985?

DID YOU KNOW?
Supergran had a host of big name stars putting in appearances. The likes of Barbara Windsor, Bernard Cribbins and Roy Kinnear to name but a few. Legendary actor Patrick Troughton's final TV appearance was in *Supergran* as he sadly died (or *failed to regenerate*) at a Doctor Who convention shortly after.

THE FLINTSTONES

The Flintstones, they really were a page right out of history, albeit an anachronistic one. For instance, they celebrated Christmas in spite of the fact they were living long before the Big J was even around! But it didn't matter and we loved their so-called mod-cons, such as cameras with little birds inside carving out images, the foot powered motor cars, and the octopus dishwasher. Here's some 'rock-hard' questions about the show, if you get stuck just shout *Wiiiiiillllllmmmaaaaaaa!* Not that it will help.

851. In the opening titles, what does Fred slide down - a mammoth's tusk or a dinosaur's tail?

852. In which town did the Flintstones live - Bedrock or Boulder?

853. Name their purple household pet dinosaur (a Snorkasaurus) - Dicky or Dino?

854. What was their pet sabre toothed tiger called - Baby-Puss or Fangles?

855. What was Barney's surname?

856. In which year did the show first air - 1955, 1960, 1965 or 1970?

857. Name the two children who eventually got their own show.

858. Was Fred's boss at the quarry called Mr Slate, Mr Granite or Mr Rockville?

859. Was the occasional little green alien called Nizbar, Buzby or Gazoo?

860. Do you remember Fred's nonsensical, excitedly bellowed catchphrase?

DID YOU KNOW?
The original title for the show was The Flagstones. *The Flintstones* is based on the American family sitcom *The Hooneymooners* which, in turn, is regarded as the basis for such shows as *The Simpsons* and *Family Guy*.
The appearance of the little green, pompous alien – trapped in the stone age - is considered to be the point where *The Flintstones* 'jumped the shark'.

SOOTY

Sooty, the little yellow glove puppet bear with a black nose and ears who could be charming one minute and a little sod the next. The puppet was found in 1948 in a Blackpool junk shop by Harry Corbett who bought it for his young son Matthew. The bear was originally all yellow so Harry made his nose and ears black with soot so the puppet would show up better on black and white TV, hence his name Sooty.

861. Harry and Sooty were regulars on which 1950s' show Saturday Special or Weekend Larfs?

862. What was Sooty's catchphrase magical spell, usually uttered by his human helper?

863. Name Sooty's squeaky, not-that-bright, canine chum.

864. What type of bear was Sooty's girlfriend Soo?

865. Was the occasionally villainous dog character called Scrap, Butch, or Tyrone?

866. What make of small van was the Sooty Mobile - Yamaha, Honda or Suzuki?

867. In which year did Matthew take over Sooty on TV - 1970, 1976 or 1980?

868. Matthew retired from his bear handling duties in 1990, 1998 or 2003?

869. Was the 1999 show set in a hotel called Sooty Heights or Sooty Towers?

870. In which SMTV sketch did Sooty get drunk on a stag night?

DID YOU KNOW?
The *Steptoe and Son* actor Harry H. Corbett put the H into his name to avoid being confused with Harry Corbett. Harry Corbett, who sadly died in 1989, was the nephew of fish and chip shop mogul Harry Ramsden. Matthew Corbett was originally one of the three singers on *Rainbow* but left to take over the Sooty Show from his dad, and Rod, Jane and Freddy were born. Harry and Matthew, you made kids' telly magical and we salute you both!

I DON'T REMEMBER THAT! (7)

10 more shows to get your childhood memories flowing which will lead to you racking your brains trying to remember people from school. Or sweets you can't get anymore. Oh bugger ... Texan bars! Bazooka Joes! Space Dust!

Which show ...

871.   Had the late Charlotte Coleman playing a thoroughly unruly girl whom her parents and her social worker Mrs Allgood try desperately to tame? ITV 1982 - 1983 although there was a previous one-off and a later series.

872.   Was quite a gloomy cartoon about a 'thing' that lived under a crack in someone's kitchen? It had a head, a mop of ginger hair and no body, just arms and legs. And an unpronounceable name. Channel 4 1981.

873.   Was a kind of animation magazine show with a mute pink cat as the anchor? The titles had a kid in a pink sports car and a brill theme song. Other than that it was torture to watch on a Saturday teatime as it kept us waiting for *Dr Who!* BBC 1969.

874.   Had the fabulous Beryl Reid *(1919–1996)* and Stephen Boxer explaining how things were on planet Earth to a puppet named Mooncat and looking at VT about the subject through the Moon Machine? Mooncat was operated by David Claridge who later did Roland Rat. ITV 1981.

875.   Saw the future Earth forced back into an almost medieval lifestyle after an alien takeover and humans given cranial implant caps to control them? This ambitious BBC sci-fi serial saw three boys fighting these never seen E.T.s in their huge, lumbering, three legged metal machines. 1984.

876. Became a benchmark in children's art, crafts and make 'n' do formats primarily due to the fantastic '*big-brother-you-always-wanted*' presenter Neil Buchanan? ITV 1989 – 2007.

877. Was about a jumbo jet made wrongly because the engineer who made him (*cheap Polish labour presumably*) mistook inches for centimetres? The result was this small, animated aeroplane. BBC 1985-86.

878. Began as part of the 1962 The Hanna-Barbera New Cartoon series along with a couple of other 'toons? This one was repeatedly shown on its own over the years and was about a brave, sword wielding turtle who righted wrongs along with his kindly dog friend Dum Dum, who was voiced by Alan 'Fred Flintsone' Reid.

879. Featured Angus and Elspeth, young siblings who were friends with a clan of monsters in Loch Ness? Their dad, Mr McTout, was the loch keeper but unfortunately never got to meet the friendly monsters. Cartoon. BBC1 1984.

880. Concerned a Swiss orphan girl who goes to live with her *bit-of-a-git* grandfather in the Alps? She befriends Peter the goatherd and her Gramps becomes less-of-a-git. There have been many adaptations of this story, but this one was dubbed into English and from 1978 onwards it was played largely in the summer hols. 26 episodes, BBC.

PADDINGTON

Produced by FilmFair, this was another hit BBC short with basic stop frame animation, a wonderfully catchy theme tune, and a bucket load of charisma and charm. Paddington was always kind, polite and well meaning, even though his good intentions caused more trouble for his devoted family than they could ever have dreamed of. And woe betide anyone who was rude to Paddington or his family for he would cast them one of his 'hard stares' causing them great embarrassment. Obviously this was a much gentler time because staring at anyone in the 21st century will get you happy slapped into intensive care, regardless of whether you're a cute anthropomorphic bear or not.

881. Paddington Bear was found at Victoria Train Station - true or false?

882. From which country did Paddington come from - India or Peru?

883. What is Paddington's favourite sandwich filling, peanut butter or marmalade?

884. And where upon his person did Paddington often keep a sandwich?

885. He is taken in by which family - the Green, the Brown or the White family?

886. Can you recall the name of their old fashioned housekeeper - was it Mz Bee or Mrs Bird?

887. Was their address 1313 Mockingbird Lane or 32 Windsor Gardens?

888. Which wonderful British actor narrated the show - John Le Mesurier or Sir Michael Horden?

889. Paddington wore a duffel coat - true or false?

890. In what year did the show begin - 1969, 1973, 1975 or 1979?

DID YOU KNOW?
The creator of Paddington is Michael Bond (a former cameraman on *Blue Peter*) who got the idea when he spotted a solitary toy bear for sale in a London shop window and bought it. The incident inspired him to write books about the lost little bear character and the first was published in 1958 entitled *A Bear Called Paddington*.

HE-MAN AND THE MASTERS OF THE UNIVERSE

He-Man might have had one of the cheesiest names ever in the history of superheroes, but it truly was 'rush home from school' telly. He was a big, muscle bound bloke who actually smacked the bad guys with some cool cartoon violence. Just what you needed after a hard day at school being pushed around by big, muscle bound P.E. teachers. And if you feel you can't answers any of these questions, simply throw back your head and shout 'I have the power!' Then cheat.

891. Who gives He-Man his powers - The Enchantress, The Sorceress or The She-Witch?

892. In which mystical castle does she reside - Castle Saburac or Castle Grayskull?

893. He-Man was his super alter-ego, but what was his normal name - Prince Valiant or Prince Adam?

894. What must he say before he can transform into He-Man?

895. What does the cowardly green tiger Cringer turn into - Fearless Feline or Battle Cat?

896. What planet was He-Man the champion and defender of - Eternia or Infinitersa?

897. Queen Marlena is the female ruler, is the King called Randor or Del'Boycey?

898. Who leads the evil Masters Of The Universe, The Mekon, Slartibartfast or Skeletor?

899. Does this villain live in Snake Mountain, The Bone Zone, or Wolf Mansion?

900. Name the fatherly inventor who is also in charge of the realm's armoury - is it Man-at-Arms or The Armoury Keeper?

DID YOU KNOW?
He-Man, unlike most merchandising franchises, didn't begin life as a TV show, it was originally a line of action figures produced by Mattel in 1981. Comics soon followed before the original animated TV series began in 1983 produced by Filmation. The series featured stories and scripts written by future *Babylon 5* creator J. Michael Straczynski.

CAPTAIN SCARLET

A lone assassin stalks a deserted backstreet. A bottle being kicked over makes him spin around and a shadowy figure becomes illuminated – it's Captain Scarlet. The assassin lets him have it with a round of machine gun fire. Scarlet doesn't even blink. Instead he raises his gun and meets out justice in the guise of one bullet to the would-be killer. Simply the most exciting and haunting opening to a TV show ever, and all narrated by the silver voiced Ed Bishop (1932 – 2005). Long before Captain Jack Harkness made being indestructible fashionable, Captain Scarlet was at it. Saving the Earth from emotionless, unseen aliens was one hell of a weekly task, but the Cap made it look effortlessly cool.

901. Which organisation does Captain Scarlet work for, WASP or Spectrum?

902. Name the airborne Head Quarters of the organisation - Cloudbase or Nimbus H.Q.

903. Was Captain Scarlet's boss Colonel White, General Grey or Major Mauve?

904. Is Captain Scarlet's real name John Taylor, Lee Henman or Paul Metcalfe?

905. Name the alien baddies of the show - the Cylons, the Vogons, or the Mysterons?

906. On which planet do the humans and aliens first encounter one another - Jupiter, Neptune, or Mars?

907. Which Captain is Captain Scarlet's arch enemy - Captain Shadow or Captain Black?

908. Which actor voiced Scarlet - Francis Matthews, Roger Moore or Paul Darrow?

909. What were the all female pilots collectively codenamed - Angels, Sirens, or Fembots?

910. Did Gerry Anderson make Captain Scarlet before, or after, *Thunderbirds*?

DID YOU KNOW?
In the opening episode mankind mistakes an alien greeting for a threat and gets in the first assault. Thus the basis for the entire conflict is based on a mistake, not unlike how the Earth Minbari War came about in *Babylon 5*. Ed Bishop provided the voice of Captain Blue and went to star in another Gerry Anderson hit *UFO (1970)*.

JACKANORY

Once upon a time, in a far off land called 1965, there was a man called Michael Peacock who had a really important job. He was Head Of Programmes for BBC2. Michael was very worried. He said to producer Joy Whitby, 'Help! We've got 15 minutes of airtime to fill, whatever shall we do?' 'Hmmm,' said Joy, 'I'll ask my chums.' And so Joy skipped along to see her friends Anna Holme and Molly Cox, at the Play School, and they came up with the idea of telling stories in the slot. But, they couldn't for the life of them think of a title for their new show. Then they half remembered a nursery rhyme they'd heard as little girls which went something like...
I'll tell you a story of Jackanory, and now my story's begun. I'll tell you another of Jack and his brother and now my story is done.
'Smashing, Jackanory it is then,' they declared. Lots of famous and important people came along to read many wonderful stories and they all lived happily ever after. Until the show was cancelled in 1996.

Now children, can you match the reader with the story they read?

	STORY READER	STORY
911.	Rik Mayall (1989)	Mrs Pepperpot
912.	HRH Prince Charles (1984)	Charlie and the Chocolate Factory
913.	Tom Baker (1986)	The Old Man of Lochnagar
914.	Spike Milligan (1984)	George's Marvellous Medicine
915.	Sheila Steafel (1981)	The Iron Man
916.	Arthur Lowe (1976)	Annerton Pit
917.	Patrick Stewart (1977)	The Three Toymakers
918.	Thora Hird (1986)	Supergran
919.	Patrick Troughton (1973)	The Emperor's Oblong Pancake
920.	Michael Palin (1986)	Help I'm a Prisoner in a Toothpaste Factory

DID YOU KNOW?
Velvet voiced Bernard Cribbins presented *Jackanory* the most times clocking up a spell binding 111 episodes, whilst the mesmerising Kenneth Williams treated us to 69 fun filled shows. Prince Charles read a story he wrote himself, and Rik Mayall's anarchic performance caused a storm of protest from outraged parents.

MAGPIE

Magpie was designed to be ITV's cooler and trendier answer to *Blue Peter*, and by Mick Robertson's curly locks it was! Mick was smoother than velvet dipped in melted Milky Ways and the unbelievably gorgeous Jenny Hanley gave many a young lad his first crush. Or perhaps you're a tad older and remember the braless Susan Stranks sporting a rather eye catching pair of Dimmocks? *Magpie* was a fun, sparky, twice weekly treat. Even the theme tune was cool and catchy. Based on a superstitious rhyme, it was warbled by The Spencer Davies Group, but the original lyrics were changed for the show. The last three were originally *'Eight for heaven, Nine for hell, Ten is for the devil himself'*. Can you match the number with what it was for? These are the changed TV lyrics by the way.

921.　One　　　　　For A Boy

922.　wo　　　　　A Secret Never To Be Told

923.　Three　　　　To Wish

924.　Four　　　　Is A Bird Never To Be Missed

925.　Five　　　　For Sorrow

926.　Six　　　　　For Silver

927.　Seven　　　　For A Girl

928.　Eight　　　　To Kiss

929.　Nine　　　　For Joy

930.　Ten　　　　　For Gold

DID YOU KNOW?
The original *Magpie* presenters were Pete Brady, Susan Stranks and Tony Bastaple. Other presenters were Douglas Rae and Tommy Boyd, but it's Mick and Jenny who stole the show.
Made by Thames Television the series ran from 1968 – 1980 and the magpie seen in the opening titles was nicknamed Murgatroyd.

I DON'T REMEMBER THAT! (8)

More shows for you to suddenly remember and blurt out 'I loved that show!' before realising you rarely actually saw it.

Which show ...

931. Was one of the first pre-school shows and featured an awkward moving wooden half donkey/half horse? It staggered about on the piano of the legendary Annette Mills, brother of the equally legendary Sir John Mills. Black and white. BBC 1946 – 1952.

932. Saw the ups and downs of the terrible junior football team the Glipton Giants and their Geordie manager Jossy Blair? Only 10 episodes were made of this classic sitcom. It was written by sports commentator Sid Waddell and had an incredibly catchy theme tune too. BBC 1986.

933. Boasted the voice talents of the legendary Peter 'Captain Pugwash' Hawkins? It was about a space boy and his little alien friend who zoomed around the galaxy in Space Freighter 9. Not really animation, the camera slowly panned over static drawings. BBC 1963 – 1977.

934. Followed a group of children trying to get home after being cast into a dangerous realm of sword and sorcery via an enchanted amusement park ride? Don 'Ralph Malph' Most voiced the cowardly Eric. Animation, BBC 1984.

935. Starred a little plasticine man whose career began with Tony Hart? He got this, his first spin off show in 1981. He lived in an art-box and had a cheeky friend called Chaz. Made by Aardman, BBC.

936. Gave us the catchphrase '*I'll skweem and skweem until I'm sick*' delivered with relish by the wonderful Bonnie Langford? Based on the books by Richmal Crompton, this wasn't the only TV rendering of the show's central character, a naughty schoolboy and his gang The Outlaws, but Langford made it the most memorable. ITV 1977.

937. Was based on a series of books by Edgar Rice Burroughs? This animated version saw the eponymous hero battling aliens and robots in the jungle as well as trying to be faithful to the 1912 creation, and it worked. It rocked! Made by Filmation. BBC 1976.

938. Came from a wonderful 1958 book by Philippa Pearce and was dramatised three times by the BBC, 1968, 1974 and 1989? Tom's brother has measles so he is sent to live with the elderly Mrs Bartholomew for his health's sake. Tom is cut off from the world and lonely until a grandfather clock strikes thirteen and a magical, time bending, adventure begins in a beautiful garden.

939. Boasted *the* smallest consulting detective in the history of animation. He was tiny! Along with his dog Braveheart, his niece Lori and her bloke Gator, he represented the Finkerton Detective Agency? Voiced by the late great Lennie Weinrib who was also H.R Pufnstuf, Scrappy Doo and a Smurf. Hanna-Barbera, BBC, 1973.

940. Was about a bunch of wholesome American kids solving mysterious crimes? Frankie, J.R., Doc, Joanne, Lil' Bill and Boomer the dog left their red painted handprints wherever they'd been. *Little House on the Prairie* star Matthew Laborteaux played Frankie and the actor playing Doc was called, believe it or not, James Bond the third. BBC 1977.

MR BENN (1)

Created by author and illustrator David McKee, Mr Benn is one of the most fondly remembered children's cartoons of all time. Mr Benn, a seemingly normal city gent, would visit the fancy dress shop once a week, get changed into a costume, then go through a magic door to find himself in an adventure to match his clothes. He would always return home at the end of the episode with a small reminder of his experience.

941. When he was himself, what type of hat did Mr Benn wear?

942. What type of hat did the shopkeeper wear?

943. What street did Mr Benn live on - Jubilation Gardens or Festive Road?

944. Can you remember the number of his house - was it 13, 40 or 52?

945. In what year was the show first broadcast - 1966, 1971 or 1978?

946. Was the smooth voiced actor who narrated the show Paul Nicholas or Ray Brooks?

947. *Not* a costume worn in the series - Cook, Fireman, Diver.

948. In *Big Game Hunter*, what did Mr Benn use to shoot animals?

949. Did the shopkeeper have a moustache?

950. In the '70s, 130 episodes of Mr Benn were made - true or false?

DID YOU KNOW?
Mr Benn began as a series of books, the first being *Mr Benn – The Red Knight* published in 1967. Creator David McKee also gave us the cartoon *King Rollo*. Mr Benn's business suited look was inspired by the famous photograph The Business Man by Micaela Mitchell.
Mr Benn never had a first name.
The phrase *'As if by magic, the shopkeeper appeared'* can still be used sarcastically when one is trying to find an assistant in most modern retail outlets staffed by gormless morons.

MR BENN (2) – MEMENTOS

Mr Benn always took home a memento of his magical adventure which seemed to prove he wasn't just imagining what happened beyond the magic door. See if you can match the 10 mementos to 10 of the characters Mr Benn dressed up as.

	MEMENTO	CHARACTER
951.	A Jolly Roger	The Clown
952.	A medal	The Zoo-Keeper
953.	A shell	The Spaceman
954.	A stone hammer	The Pirate
955.	A sheriff's badge	The Cook
956.	A box of matches	The Diver
957.	A wooden spoon	The Caveman
958.	A red nose	The Cowboy
959.	A bird's feather	The Balloonist
960.	A piece of rock	The Red Knight

DID YOU KNOW?
One of David Mckee's original Mr Benn books was never made into a *Mr Benn* cartoon. *123456789 Benn* saw the eponymous hero go to jail and share a cell with a con called Smasher Lagru. Perhaps it's just as well, one can only imagine what mementos he would have brought back from prison, a mullet haircut and an armful of badly drawn tattoos perhaps?

DO NOT ADJUST YOUR SET

The phrase 'Way ahead of it's time' is festooned far too liberally when speaking of classic TV, but *Do Not Adjust Your Set* really was. This 1960s' ITV sketch show was, along with the adult *At Last The 1948 Show*, one of the forerunners of Monty Python. Indeed, three of its cast and writers were fledgling Pythons honing their craft. *D.N.A.Y.S.* really was amazingly intellectual and surreal in places for a kids' show, but even today is laugh-out-loud funny. Sketches, spoof interviews, V.T. vignettes and musical interference from the impossibly barking English loonies The Bonzo Dog Doo-Dah Band, this classic cut of children's telly is well worth a look and is available on DVD.

961.   *Not* a star of *D.N.A.Y.S.*, Eric Idle, John Cleese, Michael Palin, Terry Jones.

962.   Was the only female cast member, Irene Handle or Denise Coffey?

963.   How many series were made - two, three, four or five?

964.   Name the fourth male cast member who was never a Python, but is equally legendary (and cushty).

965.   Did the show run 1961-1963, 1964-1966 or 1967-1969?

966.   Which Goodies star once stood in when one of the future Pythons was ill?

967.   Which Bonzo Dog star would become a Rutle - Vivian Stanshall or Neil Innes?

968.   Did Neil Innes later play a wizard in Magic Street, Puddle Lane or Diagon Alley?

969.   Was the bowler hat wearing detective character called Captain Fantastic, Inspector Spectre or Mr Lawman?

970.   What was his evil female nemesis called - Miss Terry, Mz Fizz, or Mrs Black?

DID YOU KNOW?
Vivian Stanshall, lead singer and all round musician in the Bonzo Dog Doo-Dah Band, tragically died in a house fire in 1995 caused by faulty wiring. A genuine English eccentric, Stanshall once staged a fake fight with Keith Moon in a tailor's shop over a pair of trousers which they ripped in two. A one legged actor then came in and told the horrified tailor the one legged trousers were just what he was looking for and bought them both. Mr Stanshall you were magnificent and we salute you, sir.

BATMAN – THE TV SERIES, ALSO RAN VILLAINS

We all know the big four when it comes to Batman's adversaries, The Joker (*Cesar Romero*), The Riddler (*Frank Gorshin, John Astin*), The Penguin (*Burgess Meredith*) and Catwoman (*Julie Newmar, Eartha Kitt, Lee Meriwether*), but how many of the other Gotham City felons can you remember? Match the big name actor to the lesser known Batman villain.

	VILLAIN	**ACTOR**
971.	Mr Freeze	Maurice Evans
972.	King Tut	Zsa Zsa Gabor
973.	The Bookworm	Liberace
974.	Egghead	Michael Rennie
975.	Minerva	Joan Collins
976.	The Sandman	Roddy McDowall
977.	Ma Parker	Vincent Price
978.	The Siren	Shelley Winters
979.	Fingers	George Sanders
980.	The Puzzler	Victor Buono

DID YOU KNOW?
All of these actors played their roles in Batman with relish and put the 'amp into camp', to coin a phrase no one will ever use again.
Interestingly, the wonderful Roddy McDowell (1928 -1998) and Maurice Evans (1901 – 1989) both starred in one of the greatest sci-fi films ever made, *Planet of the Apes* (1968). Roddy played Cornelius the chimp and Maurice was the crusty Dr Zaius, the orang-utan. Both these English actors were shining examples of versatility and quality and gave us so many dazzling TV, stage and film performances. We salute them both!

THE LEGEND OF BRIAN CANT

You couldn't possibly write anything about classic children's television without mentioning the guv'nor himself, Brian Cant. Born in Ipswich, Brian has given us countless hours of his performing talents and brought to life the classic Trumptonshire Trilogy of programmes *Camberwick Green* (1966), *Trumpton* (1967) and *Chigley* (1969.) He also presented *Play School* and *Play Away* as well as many other children's programmes. Brian, we salute you, sir!

981. In what year was Brian born 1923, 1933, or 1943?

982. In *Trumpton*, what was Police Constable McGary's number - 451, 452 or 453?

983. Name the last fireman, Pugh!, Pugh!, Barney McGrew!, Cuthbert!, Dibble!, ----?

984. Name the cider swilling miller from *The Trumptonshire Trilogy* - was it Cyril Cereal, Windy Miller, or Tiddly Quernstone.

985. Did Play Away run from 1971 – 1984, or 1974 – 1987?

986. Brian has presented *It's a Knockout!* - true or false?

987. Was Brian's 1998 show *Dappledown Farm* or *Duckdown Farm*?

988. In *Bric-a-Brac* (1980) what kind of shop did Brian run? - a furniture outlet, a builder's merchant or a junk shop?

989. How many episodes of *Bric-a-Brac* were made - 12, 67 or 360?

990. Was the spoof show he narrated for Lee and Herring called *The Organ Gang* or *The Trouser Snakes*?

DID YOU KNOW?
Brian is an accomplished actor and has appeared in many TV productions including *Z-Cars*, *Doctor Who*, *Doctors*, *Ever Decreasing Circles* and *Casualty* to name but a few. He's married to Cherry Britton, the sister of the wonderful Fern Britton.
There was only one series each of *Camberwick Green*, *Trumpton* and *Chigley* and only 13 episodes in each one.

DOWN THE BACK OF
THE MEMORY SOFA

These are shows that may well have never had more than one airing, or at least not one for a few decades, so it'd be unfair trying to get you to remember them. They have slipped too far down the back of your memory sofa!

So, we'll remind you of the shows, then ask you to match them with their writers – ha, that'll learn ya!

THE CLIFTON HOUSE MYSTERY was a spooky six part drama about a family who moved into a house in Clifton haunted by a dead soldier whose body they found in a sealed room. ITV 1978.

ANIMAL KWACKERS was a Yorkshire Television lunchtime show featuring men in glam-rock animal suits who sang songs and told stories. There was Rory the lion, Bongo the dog, Twang the monkey and Boots the eye patch wearing tiger. ITV 1975.

BELLE AND SEBASTIAN was a black and white French show, dubbed into English. It was about a small boy and his dog and their adventures in the Alps and was largely shown in the summer holidays. BBC 1970s.

SKY was an eerie seven episode drama about a young time traveller from another dimension trying to find the Juganet – Stonehenge - the gateway back to his own world. ITV 1975.

TUBE MICE boasted the voices of Minder stars George Cole and Dennis Waterman as animated mice – Vernon, Toaster, Squeak and Bubble - living on the Underground at Oxford Circus. ITV 1988.

THE FLOCKTON FLYER starred a Great Western Railway locomotion train and the Carter family as they try to maintain the Flockton to Lane End branch railway. ITV 1977.

SPORT BILLY was a cartoon promoting sportsmanship. A young boy from planet Olympus ruled by Sporticus *(you reading this in Lazy Town?)* travelled around the Earth, and through time, in an alarm clock shaped ship. He, his friend Lilly, and dog Willy, had to thwart the plans of the spoilsport Queen Vanda. BBC 1979.

DARK SEASON starred a pre-fame Kate Winslet and was a sci-fi drama about Marcie, a teenage girl, who becomes suspicious when the unearthly Mr Eldritch gives out free computers to every kid in school. *Blake's 7* star Jacqueline Pearce popped up in episode four. BBC 1991.

ROBERT'S ROBOTS saw mild mannered Robert Sommerby living with his Aunt Millie and a gang of malfunctioning robots. They were supposed to pass for humans but were rubbish at it, and foreign spies kept trying to steal them. ITV 1973.

THE PAPER LADS was a drama set in Newcastle about a group of paper delivery kids. It had a brilliant, folk rock theme called Back Home Once Again sung by Renaissance, but only ran for seven episodes. A sequel called News of the Paper Lads emerged a year later, but it also failed to shine. ITV 1977.

Okay dokey – it's shot in the dark time. Match the shows with their writers. (writers are the undervalued, underpaid saps who create all these wonderful shows, just in case you didn't know.)

991.	*The Clifton House Mystery*	Russell T. Davies
992.	*Animal Kwackers*	Peter Whitbread
993.	*Belle and Sebastian*	Bob Block
994.	*Sky*	Gerry Cowan
995.	*Tube Mice*	Dan Farson and Harry Moore
996.	*The Flockton Flyer*	Cecile Aubry
997.	*Sport Billy*	J.G. Holland
998.	*Dark Season*	Arthur Nadel (writer/editor)
999.	*Robert's Robots*	Bob Baker and Dave Martin
1000.	*The Paper Lads*	Simon and Sara Bor

ANSWERS

A PLETHORA O' PUPPETS

	PUPPET	HUMAN
1.	Nookie Bear	Roger De Courcey
2.	Gordon the Gopher	Phillip Schofield
3.	Lord Charles	Ray Alan
4.	Sooty	Mathew Corbett
5.	Orville the Duck	Keith Harris
6.	Lambchop	Shari Lewis
7.	Posh Paws	Noel Edmonds
8.	Zig and Zag	Chris Evans
9.	Ed the Duck	Andi Peters
10.	Basil Brush	Roy North

RENTAGHOST

11. Timothy Claypole
12. Molly Weir
13. Fred Mumford
14. The Perkins
15. Dobbin
16. If your mansion house needs haunting just call Rentaghost
17. 1976
18. 1984
19. Harold Meaker
20. Coronation Street

SWAP SHOP

21. Multi-Coloured Swap Shop
22. Swaporama
23. 146
24. John Craven
25. Eric
26. Posh Paws is an anagram of Swap Shop
27. 1982
28. Brown Sauce
29. I Wanna be a Winner
30. False, but they used to be husband and wife

THE MUPPET SHOW

31. Kermit The Frog and Miss Piggy
32. Pigs In Space
33. Veterinarians' Hospital
34. Waldorf and Statler
35. Swedish. The Swedish Chef
36. Fozzie

37.	Beaker
38.	120 episodes
39.	Sweetums
40.	John Wayne

COSGROVE HALL

41.	Jamie
42.	David Jason
43.	Rainbow
44.	The B.F.G – Big Friendly Giant
45.	Ant and Dec
46.	Andy Pandy
47.	Richard E. Grant (Jacobi played an android Master)
48.	Richard Briers
49.	Creepy Crawlies
50.	Captain Kremmen

WHOSE VOICE IS THAT? (1)

51.	The Trapdoor (1984)	Willie Rushton
52.	Mary, Mungo and Midge (1969)	Richard Baker
53.	Bod (1975)	John Le Mesurier
54.	Funny Bones (1992)	Griff Rhys Jones
55.	The Wind in the Willows (1984)	Ian Carmichael
56.	Bob the Builder (1999)	Neil Morrissey
57.	The Mr Men (1975)	Arthur Lowe
58.	The Animals of Farthing Wood (1992)	Ron Moody
59.	Raggy Dolls (1987)	Neil Innes
60.	Fireman Sam (1985)	John Alderton

HAPPY DAYS

61.	Rock Around The Clock by Bill Hailey
62.	Henry Winkler
63.	Heeeeey!
64.	False, it was set in Milwaukee
65.	Richie Cunningham
66.	Ralph Malph
67.	Suzi Quatro
68.	Arnold's
69.	1974
70.	1984

HAPPY DAYS SPIN OFF SHOWS

| 71. | Laverne and Shirley (1976 – 1983) |
| 72. | A glove |

73.   Lenny and Squiggy
74.   Robin Williams (*Mork and Mindy 1978 – 1982*)
75.   Ork
76.   An egg
77.   Nan-nu Nan-nu
78.   Orson
79.   *Joanie Loves Chachi*
80.   *The Fonz and The Happy Days Gang (1980 – 1982)*

THE GHOSTS OF MOTLEY HALL

81.   Sir George Uproar
82.   Peter Sallis
83.   Mr Gudgin
84.   Arthur English
85.   A duck pond
86.   Three
87.   The White Lady
88.   Sir Francis 'Fanny' Uproar
89.   Matt
90.   Sir Humphrey was knelt on by an elephant

ANIMAL SHOWS: PAWS AND EFFECT

91.   *Johnny Morris (1916 – 1999)*
92.   *Daktari*
93.   *Skippy The Bush Kangaroo (1966 – 1968)*
94.   *Rolf Harris*
95.   A bear
96.   *The Really Wild Show (full run was 1986 – 2006)*
97.   *Woof!*
98.   Collie
99.   *Tales of the Riverbank*, Hammy Hamster was NOT the name of the show
100.   *Alberto Frog and his Amazing Animal Band* (BBC)

DIFF'RENT STROKES

101.   Gary Coleman
102.   Wha'choo talkin' 'bout, Willis?
103.   Willis
104.   True, they had three during the course of the series.
105.   Phillip
106.   New York
107.   1978
108.   1986
109.   Janet Jackson

110.   Diff'rent folks

HANNA-BARBERA
111.   *Hong Kong Phooey (1974)*
112.   *The Flintstones (1960)*
113.   *The Yogi Bear Show (1961)*
114.   *The Smurfs (1981)*
115.   *Top Cat (1961)*
116.   *Help...It's the Hair Bear Bunch! (1971)*
117.   *Josie and the Pussycats (1970)*
118.   *Speed Buggy (1973)*
119.   *Captain Caveman and the Teen Angels (1977)*
120.   *Huckleberry Hound (1958)*

FINGERBOBS
121.   *Watch with Mother*
122.   1972
123.   *Yoffy*
124.   *Play School*
125.   False, only 13 were made
126.   *Gulliver*
127.   Flash
128.   Canadian
129.   Scampi
130.   Must do

I DON'T REMEMBER THAT! (1)
131.   *Eerie Indiana*
132.   *Timeslip*
133.   *Pipkins*
134.   *Pingu*
135.   *Jonny Briggs*
136.   *The White Horses*
137.   *Michael Bentine's Potty Time*
138.   *The Spooks of Bottle Bay*
139.   *King Rollo*
140.   *A Handful of Songs*

DOCTOR WHO – THE CLASSIC SERIES
141.   Gallifrey
142.   Bessie
143.   William Hartnell, Jon Pertwee played Doctor number three
144.   Baker. Tom Baker and Colin Baker
145.   Doctor number seven

146. United Nations Intelligence Taskforce, or U.N.I.T

147. True

148. The Master

149. Zygons

150. Cybermen

MAID MARIAN AND HER MERRY MEN

151. The Sheriff Of Nottingham

152. Barrington

153. Tailor

154. Guy of Gisbourne

155. Little Ron

156. True

157. Gary and Graeme

158. King John

159. 1989

160. Four

THOMAS THE TANK ENGINE

161. Blue

162. Sodor

163. The Fat Controller

164. False, it was Reverend W.V. Awdrey

165. A really useful engine

166. 1984 – 1990

167. True

168. Number 1

169. Irving

170. 1945

GAMESHOWS – WIN SOME TAT

171. Screen Test

172. On Safari (catchphrase: Safari-so-goody!)

173. Runaround

174. Fun House

175. Cheggers Plays Pop

176. The Adventure Game

177. Blockbusters

178. The Crystal Maze

179. It's a Knockout

180. Knightmare

BLUE PETER

181. Valerie Singleton   1962

182.	Anthea Turner	1992
183.	John Noakes	1965
184.	Matt Baker	1999
185.	Caron Keating	1986
186.	Peter Purves	1967
187.	Janet Ellis	1983
188.	Christopher Trace	1958
189.	John Leslie	1989
190.	Yvette Fielding	1987

BLUE PETER APPEALS

191.	1964 Silver paper	For guide dogs
192.	1965 Wool	For a tractor for Uganda
193.	1966 Old books	For the Lifeboat Association
194.	1969 Toy cars	For an old people's bus
195.	1970 Spoons and forks	For three caravans for under privileged kids
196.	1971 Pillowcases and socks	For a Kenyan boys' dormitory
197.	1972 Scrap metal	For an old people's centre
198.	1981 Used stamps	For water purification equipment in Java
199.	1985 Old keys	For children's hearing aids
200.	1989 Old tin cans	For baby unit apparatus

TIMMY MALLETT

201.	Wide Awake Club
202.	Wacaday
203.	Mallett's Mallet
204.	Magic
205.	Mike Myers
206.	The Beeps
207.	Utterly Brilliant!
208.	Bombularina
209.	Itsy Bitsy Teeny Weeny Yellow Polka Dot Bikini
210.	Timmy Towers

STUPID

211.	Marcus Brigstocke and Phil Cornwell
212.	Queen Sensible
213.	A gremlin
214.	Purple with an orange suit
215.	His tail
216.	Bog House Rat
217.	A Tree

218. Wonderful
219. Devil Finger!
220. Dead

PLAY SCHOOL
221. Dapple
222. False. Jemima was a rag doll
223. Jeremy Irons
224. Floella Benjamin, Chloe Ashcroft and Brian Cant
225. Female
226. Big Ted and Little Ted
227. Humpty
228. Playaway
229. Round, square and arched windows
230. Tikkabilla

I DON'T REMEMBER THAT! (2)
231. Hattytown Tales
232. Junior Showtime
233. Cloppa Castle
234. Picture Box
235. Hickory House
236. Paperplay
237. Issi Noho (this side up, use no hooks)
238. Ludwig
239. Crystal Tipps and Alistair
240. Champion the Wonder Horse

GRANGE HILL (1)
241. Phil Redmond
242. 1978
243. A sausage
244. London
245. Michael Sheard
246. Just Say No
247. Samuel 'Zammo' Maguire
248. Mr Bronson's car
249. Naomi Campbell
250. Tucker's Luck

GRANGE HILL (2) TEACHER FEATURE

TEACHER	SUBJECT
251. Mr Sutcliffe	Drama
252. Mr 'Bullet' Baxter	P.E.

253.	Miss Moony	English
254.	Mr McCartney	Music
255.	Miss Booth	Art
256.	Mr Bronson	French
257.	Mr 'Hoppy' Hopwood	Woodwork
258.	Mr Hankin	Science
259.	Mrs McClusky	Nothing : Was Head Teacher
260.	Miss 'Sexy' Lexington	Computers

GRANGE HILL (3) WORKS EXPERIENCE PLACEMENTS

	ACTOR	TV SHOW
261.	Kim Hartman	Allo Allo
262.	Claire Buckfield	2.4 Children
263.	John Alford	London's Burning
264.	Brian Capron	Coronation Street
265.	Susan Tully	EastEnders
266.	Terri Dwyer	Hollyoaks
267.	Todd Carty	The Bill
268.	Lee Cornes	Bottom
269.	Alex Kingston	E.R.
270.	Mmoloki Chrystie	Press Gang

SPACED OUT

271.	Space Vets
272.	The Jetsons
273.	Galloping Galaxies
274.	Space Precinct
275.	K9 And Company
276.	Astro Farm
277.	Star Trek: The Animated Series
278.	Ulysses 31
279.	Terrahawks
280.	Battle of the Planets

DOCTOR WHO (2) – THE CLASSIC SERIES

	VILLAIN	HOME PLANET
281.	The Master	Gallifrey
282.	Giant Spiders	Metebelis 3
283.	Daleks	Skaro
284.	The Time Meddler	Gallifrey
285.	Cybermen	Mondas (Telos is acceptable)
286.	Sontarans	Sontar
287.	Giant Robot	Earth
288.	Ice Warriors	Mars

| 289. | Mechanoids | Mechanus |
| 290. | The Rani | Gallifrey |

WACKY RACES

	DRIVER(S)	CAR NAMES
291.	Dick Dastardly and Muttley	The Mean Machine
292.	Peter Perfect	The Turbo Terrific
293.	The Ant Hill Mob	The Bulletproof Bomb
294.	Professor Pat Pending	The Convert-a-Car
295.	Sergeant Blast & Private Meekly	The Army Surplus Special
296.	The Slag Brothers	The Boulder Mobile
297.	Lazy Luke and Blubber Bear	The Arkansas Chuggabug
298.	Red Max	The Crimson Haybailer
299.	The Gruesome Twosome	The Creepy Coupe
300.	Penelope Pitstop	The Compact Pussycat

PRESS GANG

311. 301.   The Junior Gazette
302.   Julia Sawalha
303.   Kenny Phillips
304.   Colin Mathews
305.   Spike Thompson
306.   Suggs from Madness
307.   Mr Sullivan
308.   43
309.   1989
310.   There are Crocodiles

WORZEL GUMMIDGE

311.   Scatterbrook Farm
312.   Ten Acre Field
313.   The Crowman
314.   His head
315.   Cup o'tea an' a slice o'cake
316.   Aunt Sally
317.   Barbara Windsor
318.   A sailing ship's figure head
319.   Dolly Clothes Peg
320.   New Zealand

I DON'T REMEMBER THAT! (3)

321.   Marine Boy
322.   Noah and Nelly in SkylArk
323.   Ace of Wands

324.   *Barnaby the Bear*
325.   *Bananaman*
326.   *Dogtanian & The Three Muskehounds*
327.   *The Flumps*
328.   *Bod*
329.   *Cockleshell Bay*
330.   *Pinky And Perky*

GERRY ANDERSON – HEROES

	SHOW	HERO
331.	*Space 1999*	**Commander Koenig**
332.	*Stingray*	**Troy Tempest**
333.	*Space Precinct*	**Patrick Brogan**
334.	*Thunderbirds*	**Scott Tracy**
335.	*Fireball XL5*	**Steve Zodiac**
336.	*U.F.O.*	**Ed Straker**
337.	*Terrahawks*	**Dr Tiger Ninestein**
338.	*Joe 90*	**Joe McClaine**
339.	*The Protectors*	**Harry Rule**
340.	*Supercar*	**Mike Mercury**

WILLO THE WISP

341.   **Kenneth Williams**
342.   **Doyley Woods**
343.   **Television Set**
344.   **Her aerial**
345.   **Mavis Cruet**
346.   **The Moog**
347.   **Carwash**
348.   **A caterpillar**
349.   **A prince**
350.   **Twit**

THE KRANKIES

351.   **Janette Tough**
352.   **Husband and wife**
353.   **1947**
354.   **Crackerjack**
355.   **The Krankies Klub**
356.   **Fan-dabi-dozi**
357.   **BBC**
358.   **Red**
359.   **Krankies TV**
360.   **Number 46**

RAINBOW

361. Up above the streets and houses, rainbow planning high.
362. Geoffrey Hayes
363. Z-Cars
364. David Cook
365. False, he just did Zippy and George.
366. A boy
367. Sang songs (and NOTHING else)
368. 1972-1992
369. Sesame Street
370. Sunshine and Moony

MAGIC MOMENTS

371. *Lizzie Dripping*
372. *Mr Majeika*
373. *T-Bag*
374. *The Worst Witch*
375. *The Box of Delights*
376. *Sabrina the Teenage Witch*
377. *Into the Labyrinth*
378. *Grotbags*
379. *The Witches and the Grinnygog*
380. *Simon and the Witch*

SCOOBY DOO (1)

381. Mystery Inc.
382. The Mystery Machine
383. Great Dane
384. Shaggy
385. Daphne Blake
386. False, it's Velma Dinkle
387. Her glasses (My glasses, I can't find my glasses!)
388. Scooby Snacks
389. Willies!
390. False, it was Casey Kasem

SCOOBY DOO (2)

391.	*Scooby Doo Where Are You?*	1969
392.	*The New Scooby-Doo Movies*	1972
393.	*The Scooby- Doo Show*	1976
394.	*Scooby-Doo and Scrappy-Doo*	1979
395.	*The All New Scooby-Doo and Scrappy-Doo Show*	1983
396.	*The 13 Ghosts of Scooby-Doo*	1985
397.	*Scooby-Doo Meets the Ghoul Brothers*	1987

398.	*A Pup Named Scooby-Doo*	1988
399.	*Scooby-Doo and the Reluctant Werewolf*	1989
400.	*What's New Scooby-Doo?*	2002

SPACE 1999

401.   Moonbase Alpha
402.   Martin Landau
403.   Eagles
404.   Barbara Baine
405.   Catherine Schell
406.   Psychon
407.   Alan Carter
408.   True
409.   48
410.   13th September 1999

THE CLANGERS

411.   1969
412.   Oliver Postgate
413.   Wool (they were knitted by the animator's wife)
414.   Blue String Pudding
415.   The Soup Dragon
416.   Froglets
417.   Whistles
418.   The Iron Chicken
419.   The Cloud
420.   27 (two series of 13 and one special)

SPONGEBOB SQUARE PANTS

421.   Bikini Bottom
422.   A pineapple
423.   The Krusty Krab
424.   False, it's Mr Eugene H. Krabs
425.   Squidward Tentacles
426.   Patrick Star
427.   Gary
428.   Sandy Cheeks
429.   Mr Plankton
430.   Patchy the Pirate

I DON'T REMEMBER THAT! (4)

431.   Spatz
432.   Moondial
433.   Budgie the Little Helicopter

434. *Mike and Angelo*
435. *A.L.F.*
436. *Children's Ward*
437. *Big John, Little John*
438. *Dodger, Bonzo and the Rest*
439. *The Woodentops*
440. *Fraggle Rock*

CAPTAIN PUGWASH

441. Horatio
442. The Black Pig
443. Master Mate
444. False, it was Tom
445. Cut-Throat Jake
446. The Flying Dustman
447. 1957
448. 86
449. Peter Hawkins
450. The Trumpet Hornpipe

TONY HART

451. *Vision On*
452. *The Gallery*
453. *Take Hart*
454. Mr Bennett
455. *Hart Beat*
456. Morph
457. The Blue Peter badge
458. Quackers
459. 1925
460. *Saturday Special* (1951 – 1953)

HERE COME THE DOUBLE DECKERS

461. Seven
462. London
463. Peter Firth
464. Sticks
465. Brains
466. Tiger
467. Doughnut
468. Melvyn Hayes
469. Spring
470. 17

BASIL BRUSH

471.   Terry Thomas
472.   David Nixon
473.   Rodney Bewes
474.   1969 – 1973
475.   1973 – 1977
476.   1979 – 1980
477.   *Let's Read with Basil Brush* (ITV 1982 – 1983)
478.   *The Weakest Link*
479.   No, but that would be **good** telly!
480.   *Swap Shop (Basil's Swap Shop)*

GET YOUR FACTS RIGHT!

481.   *John Craven's Newsround*
482.   *Ask Aspel*
483.   *The Book Tower*
484.   *Brainchild*
485.   *Clapperboard*
486.   *Think of a Number*
487.   *Record Breakers*
488.   *How*
489.   *Why Don't You? (Why don't you just switch off your television set and go and do something less boring instead?)*
490.   *Jim'll Fix It*

CRACKERJACK (1)

491.   Friday
492.   Five to five
493.   Eamonn Andrews
494.   A Crackerjack pencil (later a pen)
495.   I could crush a grape
496.   False, it was Double or Drop
497.   A cabbage
498.   Take A Chance
499.   400
500.   Chas and Dave

CRACKERJACK (2)

	PRESENTER	YEARS PRESENTED
501.	Eamonn Andrews	1955 - 1964
502.	Peter Glaze	1960 - 1979
503.	Stu Francis	1980 - 1984
504.	Ed 'Stewpot' Stewart	1975 - 1979
505.	The Krankies	1981 - 1982

506.	Don Maclean	1973 - 1976
507.	Michael Aspel	1968 - 1974
508.	Leslie Crowther	1964 - 1968
509.	Little and Large	1972 - 1972
510.	Ronnie Corbett	1957 - 1960

BANANA SPLITS

511. A beagle
512. A lion
513. Dear Drooper
514. An elephant
515. A gorilla
516. Snorky played keyboards, Bingo played drums
517. The Sour Grapes
518. By non-stop dancing messenger girls
519. The Three Musketeers
520. 31

ROOBARB

521. Green
522. A cat
523. Pink
524. The shed
525. The birds
526. Richard Briers
527. BBC1
528. 30
529. Roobarb and Custard Too
530. Bob Godfrey

TISWAS

531. Sally James
532. This is what they want!
533. Spit The Dog
534. The Phantom Flan Flinger
535. Trevor McDoughnut
536. The Four Bucketeers
537. The Bucket of Water Song
538. Today is Saturday, Watch and Smile
539. Shades
540. 302

FROM SMALL SCREEN TO BIG SCREEN

| 541. | Sponge Bob Square Pants | True |

542.	*The Double Deckers*	False
543.	*The Muppet Show*	True
544.	*Mr Benn*	False
545.	*Round The Twist*	False
546.	*Five Children And It*	True
547.	*The Monkees*	True
548.	*Rentaghost*	False
549.	*The Brady Bunch*	True
550.	*Rugrats*	True

SMTV LIVE

551.	Chums
552.	*Live and Kicking*
553.	Captain Justice
554.	Wonky Donkey
555.	Cat the Dog
556.	Challenge Ant
557.	The Postbag
558.	Dec Says, or The Secret Of My Success
559.	Fartbeat
560.	*Casually*

ANT AND DEC

561.	*Why Don't You?*
562.	*Byker Grove*
563.	Dec played Duncan
564.	Ant's character P.J.
565.	Two
566.	*(I'm Not Your) Steppin' Stone* (1996)
567.	*Ant And Dec Unzipped* (1997)
568.	*CD:UK (they presented it 1998 – 2001)*
569.	*Friends Like These* (1998)
570.	Dec usually stands on the right

STINGRAY

571.	Anything can happen in the next half hour
572.	Captain Troy Tempest
573.	James Garner
574.	Phones
575.	World Aquanaut Security Patrol
576.	Commander Sam Shore
577.	Titan
578.	True
579.	Aqua Marina

580.   39

BAGPUSS
581.   Emily
582.   Pink and white
583.   Madeline
584.   False, it was Professor Yaffle
585.   1974
586.   The banjo
587.   The Organ (The Marvellous Mechanical Mouse Organ)
588.   We will fix it! We will mend it!
589.   False (it was Oliver Postage)
590.   13

THE GOODIES
591.   Graeme
592.   Ecky Thump
593.   Buttercup
594.   The O.K. Tea Rooms
595.   Funky Gibbon (1975)
596.   Superchaps 3
597.   The Post Office Tower
598.   72
599.   The Bubblegum Brigade
600.   The Goodies in Toyland

THE MAGIC ROUNDABOUT
601.   Mr Rusty
602.   Zebedee
603.   False, it was Dylan
604.   1965
605.   Dougal and the Blue Cat
606.   Tony Hancock
607.   Robbie Williams
608.   A snail
609.   Ermintrude
610.   Nigel Planer

I DON'T REMEMBER THAT! (5)
611.   The Littlest Hobo
612.   The Storyteller
613.   Murphy's Mob
614.   Johnny and the Dead
615.   Metal Mickey

616. *The Herbs*
617. *Dramarama*
618. *Follyfoot*
619. *Little Blue*
620. *Wizbit*

BATMAN – THE TV SERIES
621. Adam West
622. Alfred
623. Dick Grayson
624. Burt Ward
625. Commissioner Gordon
626. His daughter
627. Frank Gorshin
628. Chief O'Hara
629. False, it was Cesar Romero (Meredith played The Penguin)
630. Joan Collins

TELETUBBIES
631. Eh-Oh!
632. Red
633. Noo-Noo
634. Po
635. Laa-Laa
636. Rabbits
637. Yellow
638. Ragdoll Productions
639. Green
640. 365

ROD HULL AND EMU
641. His right arm
642. No, Emu was mute
643. Emu's Broadcasting Company
644. Pink
645. Grotbags
646. Green
647. *There's somebody at the door!* (repeat)
648. Michael Parkinson
649. Snoop Dogg
650. He was 63

WHOSE VOICE IS THAT? (2)
651. *Bleep and Booster* (1963)   Peter Hawkins

652.	*Henry's Cat* (1983)	Bob Godfrey
653.	*Huxley Pig* (1989)	Martin Jarvis
654.	*William's Wish Wellingtons* (1992)	Andrew Sachs
655.	*Towser* (1982)	Roy Kinnear
656.	*Grizzly Tales for Gruesome Kids* (2000)	Nigel Planer
657.	*The Little Green Man* (1989)	Jon Pertwee
658.	*Simon in the Land of Chalk Drawings* (1974)	Bernard Cribbins
659.	*Doctor Snuggles* (1980)	Peter Ustinov
660.	*Fred Basset* (1976)	Lionel Jeffries

DANGERMOUSE

661. A post box
662. Baker Street (which is in Marylebone NOT Mayfair as the show states)
663. David Jason
664. Terry Scott
665. Baron Silas Greenback
666. Nero
667. Stiletto (full name Stiletto Mafiosa)
668. Colonel K
669. True
670. 89

THE TOMORROW PEOPLE

671. Breaking out
672. The Lab
673. London Underground station
674. Jaunting
675. TIM
676. John
677. Nicholas Young
678. *The Slaves of Jedikiah*
679. Homo-Superior
680. *Oh! You Pretty Things*

CHUCKLE BROTHERS

681. Paul and Barry
682. Rotherham
683. *New Faces*
684. *The Chucklehounds*
685. 13
686. 1987
687. To me, to you (REPEAT)
688. *To Me, To You*

689. 1996-98
690. Elliot

I DON'T REMEMBER THAT! (6)
691. *Eggs 'n' Baker*
692. *Popeye*
693. *Postman Pat*
694. *Roland Rat The Series*
695. *The Smurfs*
696. *The Baker Street Boys*
697. *Rag, Tag and Bobtail*
698. *Granddad*
699. *Sesame Street*
700. *Pob's Programme*

SATURDAY MORNING TV (1)
701.	*Going Live*	1987
702.	*Swap Shop*	1976
703.	*No. 73*	1982
704.	*Ministry of Mayhem*	2004
705.	*Tiswas*	1974
706.	*Get Fresh*	1986
707.	*Live and Kicking*	1993
708.	*Dick and Dom in Da Bunglaow*	2003
709.	*SMTV Live*	1998
710.	*The 8.15 from Manchester*	1990

SATURDAY MORNING TV (2)
711.	*Motormouth*	Neil Buchanan
712.	*No. 73*	Sandi Toksvig
713.	*Ministry of Mayhem*	Stephen Mulhern, Holly Willoughby
714.	*Going Live*	Phillip Schofield, Sarah Greene
715.	*Saturday Superstore*	Mike Reid
716.	*Parallel 9*	Mercator The Alien
717.	*Live and Kicking*	Emma Forbes, Andi Peters
718.	*SMTV Live*	Ant, Dec and Cat
719.	*Gimme 5*	Jenny Powell, Nobby the Sheep
720.	*Fully Booked*	Zoe Ball, Grant Scott

THUNDERBIRDS
721. International Rescue

722. Jeff Tracy
723. Tracy Island
724. A submarine
725. Sam
726. A space station
727. Brains
728. Lady Penelope (full name Lady Penelope Creighton-Ward)
729. Parker (full name Aloysius Parker)
730. A Rolls Royce

CHILDREN OF THE STONES

731. Astrophysicist
732. Milbury
733. Matthew
734. 53
735. 1977
736. Happy day
737. Rafael
738. Freddie Jones
739. Seven
740. ITV

FROM BIG SCREEN TO SMALL SCREEN

741.	Ace Ventura Pet Detective	True
742.	Monsters Inc	False
743.	Honey I Shrunk The Kids	True
744.	Ghostbusters	True
745.	Jumanji	True
746.	Agent Cody Banks	False
747.	The Railway Children	False
748.	The Mask	True
749.	Chitty Chitty Bang Bang	False
750.	Bigfoot and the Hendersons	True

HONG KONG PHOOEY

751. Penrod Pooch, or Penry for short
752. False, he was the janitor
753. A filing cabinet
754. Sergeant Flint
755. Spot
756. Rosemary
757. The Phooeymobile
758. By banging on a gong
759. Cat Napper was not a H.K.P. villain.

760.   *The Hong Kong Book of Kung-Fu*

THE WOMBLES
761.   Wimbledon Common
762.   Great Uncle Bulgaria
763.   Madame Cholet
764.   Bernard Cribbins
765.   Tobermory
766.   Elisabeth Beresford
767.   Orinoco
768.   *The Wombles of Wimbledon Common are we*
769.   False, he was called Wellington
770.   1973

DOCTOR WHO – THE NEW SERIES
771.   The Ninth Doctor
772.   The Time War
773.   Rose Tyler
774.   Donna Noble
775.   Sarah Jane Smith
776.   Captain Jack Harkness
777.   Sir Derek Jacobi and John Simm
778.   Astrid Peth
779.   David MacDonald
780.   Raxacoricofallapatorius

H.R. PUFNSTUF
781.   Jimmy
782.   Boat
783.   A dragon
784.   Living Island
785.   Witchiepoo *(full name Wilhelmina W.Witchiepoo)*
786.   The Vroom Broom
787.   1969
788.   Freddie
789.   John Wayne
790.   17

CATWEAZLE
791.   The 11th century
792.   Normans
793.   Carrot
794.   Owlface
795.   Nothing works

796.	1970
797.	26
798.	A toad
799.	The telling-bone
800.	Castle Saburac

TOP CAT

801.	False, he wore a flat straw boater hat.
802.	Officer Dibble
803.	New York
804.	A coin
805.	His lunch box
806.	Brain
807.	Hanna-Barbera
808.	30
809.	Mange
810.	Boss Cat

FROM PAGE TO SMALL SCREEN

811.	Stig of the Dump	True
812.	Mary Poppins	False
813.	Chocky	True
814.	Harry Potter	False
815.	Black Beauty	True
816.	The Lion, The Witch and The Wardrobe	True
817.	His Dark Materials	False
818.	Charlie and the Chocolate Factory	False
819.	Danny Champion of the World	False
820.	The Machine Gunners	True

THE SINGING RINGING TREE

821.	It will sing and ring
822.	A bear
823.	Stone
824.	A fish
825.	By freezing the lake
826.	Her beauty
827.	A musical bridge
828.	He digs out a cave
829.	Fire
830.	1959

BUTTON MOON

831.	Blanket Sky

832. Mr Spoon
833. Tina Teaspoon
834. Eggbert
835. Junk Planet
836. A baked bean tin
837. A telescope
838. Thames Television
839. Less, there were 91 episodes
840. Robin Parkinson

SUPERGRAN

841. Granny Smith
842. True
843. Willard
844. Chisleton
845. 27 (inclusive of two series and one special)
846. The Scunner Campbell
847. True
848. Billy Connolly
849. Gudrun Ure
850. 1985

THE FLINTSTONES

851. A dinosaur's tail
852. Bedrock
853. Dino
854. Baby-Puss
855. Rubble
856. 1960
857. Pebbles and Bamm-Bamm
858. Mr Slate
859. Gazoo
860. Yabba-dabba-do!

SOOTY

861. Saturday Special (1951 - 1953)
862. Izzy Wizzy Let's Get Busy!
863. Sweep
864. A panda
865. Butch
866. Suzuki
867. 1976
868. 1998
869. Sooty Heights

870.   *Chums*

I DON'T REMEMBER THAT! (7)
871.   *Educating Marmalade*
872.   *Murun Buchstansangur*
873.   *The Pink Panther Show*
874.   *Get up and Go!*
875.   *Tripods*
876.   *Art Attack*
877.   *Jimbo And The Jet Set*
878.   *Touche Turtle*
879.   *The Family Ness*
880.   *Heidi*

PADDINGTON
881.   False, he was found at Paddington Train Station
882.   Peru *(darkest Peru to be precise)*
883.   Marmalade
884.   Under his hat
885.   The Brown family
886.   Mrs Bird
887.   32 Windsor Gardens *(the other is The Munster's address)*
888.   Sir Michael Horden (1911 – 1995)
889.   True
890.   1979

HE-MAN AND THE MASTERS OF THE UNIVERSE
891.   The Sorceress
892.   Castle Grayskull
893.   Prince Adam
894.   By The Power of Grayskull
895.   Battle Cat
896.   Eternia
897.   Randor
898.   Skeletor
899.   Snake Mountain
900.   Man-at-Arms

CAPTAIN SCARLET
901.   Spectrum
902.   Cloudbase
903.   Colonel White
904.   Paul Metcalfe
905.   The Mysterons

906.	Mars
907.	Captain Black
908.	Francis Matthews
909.	Angels
910.	After, Captain Scarlet first aired in 1967

JACKANORY

911.	Rik Mayall (1989)	George's Marvellous Medicine
912.	HRH Prince Charles (1984)	The Old Man of Lochnagar
913.	Tom Baker (1986)	The Iron Man
914.	Spike Milligan (1984)	Help I'm a Prisoner in a Toothpaste Factory
915.	Sheila Steafel (1981)	Supergran
916.	Arthur Lowe (1976)	The Emperor's Oblong Pancake
917.	Patrick Stewart (1977)	Annerton Pit
918.	Thora Hird (1986)	Mrs Pepperpot
919.	Patrick Troughton (1973)	The Three Toymakers
920.	Michael Palin (1986)	Charlie and the Chocolate Factory

MAGPIE

921.	One	For Sorrow
922.	Two	For Joy
923.	Three	For A Girl
924.	Four	For A Boy
925.	Five	For Silver
926.	Six	For Gold
927.	Seven	For A Secret Never To Be Told
928.	Eight	To Wish
929.	Nine	To Kiss
930.	Ten	Is A Bird Never To Be Missed

I DON'T REMEMBER THAT! (8)

931.	Muffin the Mule
932.	Jossy's Giants
933.	Bleep and Booster
934.	Dungeons and Dragons
935.	The Amazing Adventures of Morph
936.	Just William
937.	Tarzan Lord of the Jungle
938.	Tom's Midnight Garden
939.	Inch High Private Eye
940.	The Red Hand Gang

MR BENN (1)

941. A bowler hat
942. A fez
943. Festive Road
944. 52
945. 1971
946. Ray Brooks
947. Fireman
948. A camera
949. Yes he did
950. False, only 13 episodes were made in the 70s, although a 14th episode *Mr Benn - Gladiator* was made in 2001

MR BENN (2) - MEMENTOS

	MEMENTO	CHARACTER
951.	A Jolly Roger	The Pirate
952.	A medal	The Balloonist
953.	A shell	The Diver
954.	A stone hammer	The Caveman
955.	A sheriff's badge	The Cowboy
956.	A box of matches	The Red Knight
957.	A wooden spoon	The Cook
958.	A red nose	The Clown
959.	A bird's feather	The Zoo-Keeper
960.	A piece of rock	The Spaceman

DO NOT ADJUST YOUR SET

961. John Cleese
962. Denise Coffey
963. Two
964. David Jason
965. 1967-1969
966. Tim Brooke-Taylor
967. Neil Innes
968. Puddle Lane
969. Captain Fantastic
970. Mrs Black

BATMAN – THE TV SERIES, ALSO RAN VILLAINS

	VILLAIN	ACTOR
971.	Mr Freeze	George Sanders
972.	King Tut	Victor Buono
973.	The Bookworm	Roddy McDowall
974.	Egghead	Vincent Price

975.	Minerva	Zsa Zsa Gabor
976.	The Sandman	Michael Rennie
977.	Ma Parker	Shelley Winters
978.	The Siren	Joan Collins
979.	Fingers	Liberace
980.	The Puzzler	Maurice Evans

THE LEGEND OF BRIAN CANT

981. 1933
982. 452
983. Grubb!
984. Windy Miller
985. 1971 – 1984
986. True
987. Dappledown Farm (Five)
988. A junk shop
989. 12
990. The Organ Gang

DOWN THE BACK OF THE MEMORY SOFA

991.	The Clifton House Mystery	Dan Farson and Harry Moore
992.	Animal Kwackers	Gerry Cowan
993.	Belle and Sebastian	Cecile Aubry
994.	Sky	Bob Baker and Dave Martin
995.	Tube Mice	Simon and Sara Bor
996.	The Flockton Flyer	Peter Whitbread
997.	Sport Billy	Arthur Nadel (writer / editor)
998.	Dark Season	Russell T. Davies
999.	Robert's Robots	Bob Block
1000.	The Paper Lads	J.G. Holland

REVIEWS

"At last, the definitive quiz book for classic children's telly! Now we can spend endless hours arguing with our friends and family about what colour Roobarb was, whether Hong Kong Phooey was called Henry or Penry, and of course what ever happened to Mr Bronson's wig!
Our old chum Dean has spent millions and millions of hours researching this book. Trawling the internet for facts. Ringing, emailing and blackmailing the stars of yesteryear for titbits of information. Watching DVDs and videos of every kid's show ever made – especially the bits of Tiswas where Sally James was wearing sexy boots. Actually, we heard that was the only thing he watched.
So if you have fond memories of Rent-A-Ghost, Swap Shop, Happy Days, Grange Hill and thousands of other terrific telly, then by the time you've read this book those memories will be even......fonderer.
And, after dipping into this book, you'll be able to trick your chums into saying the word Crackerjack! so you can quickly shout Crackerjack! back! By Noel Edmonds' beard this Children's TV Quiz book is a tome of boundless fun and heart warming nostalgia!
And by the way, Mr Bronson's wig is currently driving a cab, but has just written it's autobiography 'That Grumpy Bugger Was Beneath Me.'"
- Trevor and Simon

"I spent 50 years involved in children's television, and so I am delighted that Dean Wilkinson has compiled a book with 1000 questions on the subject.
Even if you are not a quiz lover, you will no doubt learn a lot about children's TV in trying to answer these questions.
Dean tells me that I am included in the quiz, and so I shall certainly read the book to see if I can answer these questions about myself!"
- Tony Hart

"Good Kid's TV is timeless. Full of fabulous characters and vibrant ideas for fertile imaginations. It is also a great place for talented actors, writers, animators, directors and producers to hone their skills.   Protecting the environment that allows these shows to be produced from today's increasingly onerous corporate financial pressures, is essential to the long term health of British TV production as a whole."
- Adam Sharp, Roobarb & Custard Too (Executive Producer)

REVIEWS

"Like Tony Hart, I too have been connected with children's television programmes for nearly 50 years, both writing and performing. It has been a great privilege to be involved with the early pioneering programmes such as Play School, Play Away and The Trumptonshire Trilogy as well as, Bric-a-Brac, Dappledown Farm and many others."
- Brian Cant

"Utterly brilliant! Dean's finally gone and done the Children's TV Quiz Book! He always said he would, and he always keeps his promises. Like the time he said he was going to conquer Iceland in the name of Her Majesty. He did too, albeit unsuccessfully, and now has to do all his shopping in Asda instead.
This book is going to bring back so many wonderful memories from a time when kid's telly was great, men were men, women were women, and puppets were puppets. Maybe it'll answer the burning question – 'Why did Bungle wear a towel when he got out of the bath, but walked around naked the rest of the time?'
So sit back, dip into the book and let your misspent childhood catch up with you once again. Now, where did I put my mallet?, I feel like bonking somebody over the head with it and screaming blaaaaaaah! in their ears."
- Timmy Mallett

"What a wonderful and entertaining trip down memory lane The Children's TV Quiz Book is. There's a veritable multitude of awe inspiring kid's TV shows that come bounding back into your memory as you flick through the pages. There's questions - some easy, some stinkers - amazing facts, fascinating trivia, and a whole heap of fun to be had here.
I always get a warm glow when someone comes up and tells me they have had many joyous hours watching Thunderbirds or Captain Scarlet or Stingray – it really makes me feel like I've done my job well. But let's keep those happy hours ticking over with more and more quality kid's telly because children today deserve happy memories of sprawling out on the couch and spending a bit of time with the old goggle box too. Save kid's TV and save the future of imagination!"
- Gerry Anderson OBE

REVIEWS

"This is a terrific and entertaining collection. I'm sure it will
become a definitive reference book on Kid's TV.
It also reminds us of the richness and variety of Kid's TV in the
UK and underlines the need to support it in the future.
Kid's TV is under real threat at present and we need to make sure
that the book which covers the next 50 years of programmes will be
as rich as this one."
- Anna Home OBE

"A book that not only tests knowledge of classic children's TV,
but brings back great memories too! A fantastic read."
- Chris Pritchard, The Severn 106.5 & 107.1 FM

"Television is probably the only culture that links us all. Dean's book is
extraordinarily well researched and is not just a quiz book, but a history
book in disguise. I enjoyed it tremendously, and I'm a crabbit old wrinkly
who's worked in TV for nigh on 40 years. You'll simply love it!"
- Tony Currie, BBC Radio Scotland 92-95 FM

"I'm a bit like Wurzel Gummidge, I had to put my thinking
head on - great fun!"
- Steve Simms, Coast 96.3 FM

"How great was it to have my memory jogged? I read,
I reminisced, I loved it!"
- Ian Burrage, Orchard 96.5 FM

"It's a book of childhood memories for all ages. You'll be taking a
trip down nostalgia avenue and sharing great TV moments with your
children as they will there's. It is fantastic fun to test yourself or your
family and friends."
- Chris Buckley, Peak 107.4 FM

REVIEWS

"This quiz book is a must for any childhood TV fan. Written with a great deal of depth and knowledge, this book is the perfect companion to any quiz night."
- Jay Curtis, Swansea Bay Radio 102.1 FM

"Brilliant ... so many forgotten memories and contrary to my parents threats, all that TV didn't make my eyes go funny after all!"
- Neil Bentley, The Severn 106.5 FM

"A must-have quiz book for all ages, it appeals to the child in us all - just pass me the liquorice shoelaces!"
- Lynne Mortimer, East Anglian Daily Times

"This is brilliant! At last, a quiz book that is as funny and entertaining as it is exasperating ... with the added ingredient of sheer nostalgia ... a classic!"
- Johnny Hero, Downtown Radio

"It's scary to think how much time I spent watching TV as a kid. School summer holiday morning memories came flooding back - waiting for the Test Card to finish before the programmes began! The book looks fab!"
- Al Duprés, KCFM 99.8 FM

"Everyone looks back with fondness on those innocent days of watching favourite TV shows. They were real treasured occasions. Here's a golden opportunity to re-live some of those classic kids' programmes. You find yourself smiling as you visualise those cherished characters and hear those tunes all over again. And the 'did you know' sections are laced with humour, wonderful nonsense and sad little ditties. Enjoy!"
- Janet Lee, Cannock Chase Post

"Baffling enough to turn a juvenile delinquent!"
- Bill McBride, The Weekly News

"Great quiz fun for all the family from one of TV's top children's writers."
- Harris Dee, Somerset County Gazette